Global Inc.

**Other Books**
by Medard Gabel

*Empty Breadbasket? The Coming Challenge to America's Food Supply and What We Can Do About It* (co-author), Rodale Press, 1982

*Ho-Ping: Food for Everyone*, Anchor Press/Doubleday, 1979

*Energy, Earth and Everyone*, Straight Arrow Books, Simon & Schuster, 1975

*Environmental Design Science Primer* (co-author), Advocate Press/Department of Health, Education, and Welfare, Division of Environmental Education, 1975

# Global Inc.
## An Atlas of the Multinational Corporation

Medard Gabel
Henry Bruner

A Visual Exploration of the History, Scale, Scope, and Impacts
of Multinational Corporations

A project of the New Global History Initiative,
the World Game Institute, and osEarth

Mapping the Multinational Corporations Project
Alfred Chandler, Harvard Business School, Co-chair
Bruce Mazlish, MIT History Department, Co-chair
Medard Gabel, World Game Institute/osEarth, Project Supervisor
Henry Bruner, World Game Institute, Project Director

THE NEW PRESS

To my wife, Mary, whose love and support made this book possible; to my children, Tobias and Zoe, whose enthusiasm and joy made it fun; and to all the other children in the world, who made it essential
—Medard Gabel

To Jim and Steve
—Henry Bruner

Published in the United States by The New Press, New York, 2003
Distributed by W. W. Norton & Company, Inc., New York

ISBN 1-56584-727-X
CIP data available

The New Press was established in 1990 as a not-for-profit alternative to the large, commercial publishing houses currently dominating the book publishing industry. The New Press operates in the public interest rather than for private gain, and is committed to publishing, in innovative ways, works of educational, cultural, and community value that are often deemed insufficiently profitable.

The New Press, 38 Greene Street, 4th Floor, New York, NY 10013
www.thenewpress.com

Book design by Ricardo E. Gálvez and Henry Bruner

Printed in Canada

2  4  6  8  10  9  7  5  3  1

# Contents

# Preface

Mapping the Multinational Corporations is a part of the effort to conceptualize and to see globalization in a historical perspective. The New Global History Initiative (http://web.mit.edu/newglobalhistory/) itself starts from the assumption that we are in what might usefully be called a "global epoch," marked by a number of factors that are transcending existing national boundaries in an intensive and extensive fashion hitherto unknown, though with deep roots in the past. Inspired by this conviction, I and my colleagues in the New Global History Initiative planned this project, so ably carried out by Medard Gabel and Henry Bruner. Among the factors making for the global epoch—and many more could be instanced—are humanity's step into space; the satellites circling the globe, making for instantaneous communications; the nuclear threat, drifting across national demarcations; the environmental danger, again manifested beyond local lines; and the spread of multinational corporations and their influence and activities. All of these factors are marked by a synergy and synchronicity new to the human experience.

Here in this work our focus is on the last named, the transnational or multinational corporations. Multinationals have been increasing almost exponentially in size and scope, as the visual representations that follow will show. It is startling to realize that, as reported by the UN (another factor in globalization?), of the 100 largest economies in the world, 53 are multinationals, which means that they are larger and wealthier on this index than 120–130 of the remaining nation-states. Their power and effect are almost incalculable in regards not only to the economy but to politics, society, and culture. They have an impact on practically every sphere of modern life, from policy making in regard to the environment and international security; from problems of identity and community; and from the future of work to the future of the nation-state.

Multinationals are, in fact, the new Leviathans of our time. It is essential that we understand their nature, purpose, historical roots, growth, and functioning. We need, literally, to "see" them in the same manner as we see the nation-states. In almost any atlas, nations are prominently displayed inside their boundaries and marked by their rivers, mountains, and cities. We need an equivalent atlas for our Leviathans, and this volume is intended to fulfill that requirement. Our intention is to portray both the static and the dynamic aspects of these powerful new institutions.

As is well known, maps were a guide to the new world of the fifteenth century; they gave a sense of direction and offered a comprehension of the areas under survey. Our maps of *Global Inc.* are not intended as guides to the visible world, as the *portolàni* used by Columbus were supposed to be; ours are more a guide to a globe and a process of globalization that is emerging both visibly and virtually. Such a mapping, for example, will show where multinationals are, and have been, headquartered; how their affiliates are scattered throughout the world; the size and location of their investments; the transborder flows of their goods and services; and so forth. They will also point to the effect of such developments on labor and work, on production and consumption, on culture, politics, and society.

In order to do all this, we needed the kind of analytic work that could frame the question of what to map, as well as a great deal of data. To this end, a conference was held. One result is a companion volume of essays to this atlas, *Multinational Corporations: The Leviathans of the New Global History* (forthcoming). That conference and resultant book supplied much of the context in which the present atlas was thought through and worked out. This *Global Inc.* atlas, however, stands as a self-contained work that illuminates the space and time in which, willy-nilly, we are all increasingly living.

The combined result of book and atlas, we hope, will be to stimulate thought about the issues surrounding the rise and expansion of multinationals, not just as business entities, but as institutions that influence social, cultural, and political conditions around the world. By providing an interdisciplinary perspective on the history, nature, and purpose of multinational corporations, we hope to help lay a rigorous foundation for constructing policies that affect these firms, and to help create an informed and diverse debate about the role that multinationals can and will play in future global developments. Such is the "global" reach of our project.

On behalf of the Toynbee Prize Foundation and its New Global History Initiative, I wish to thank the Ford Foundation and the Rockefeller Brothers Fund for their generous support of the overall project, which allowed us to organize the original conference and to commission the World Game Institute to prepare this volume—*Global Inc.*—and thus carry out our intention of giving visual representation to the multinational corporations that form so critical a part of present-day globalization.

Bruce Mazlish
MIT
2003

vi

# Foreword

Maps are attempts to capture and synthesize complexity into a form through which the human brain can interpret the information they contain; a combination of art and science leading to improved, if selective, understanding. As such, they are not an end in themselves but a tool of analysis, designed by those who seek change and progress.

This atlas provides a snapshot of the world's commercial activity at the beginning of a new century. The importance of the data captured in these pages is in no way diminished by the fact that each of the companies surveyed here has already changed. Some have gone out of existence, some have been affected by the cyclical tides of the economy, while others have grown significantly. The restless dynamism of the business world in general and of international business in particular is one of the key messages to be drawn from the atlas. In contrast to the geographical maps to which we are so accustomed, the coastlines of business are never fixed.

But change is not limited to external boundaries. There is also constant change within each individual company in response to many of the issues and challenges identified by the authors. Globalization is a force of creative disruption—challenging old patterns of economic activity, and sweeping away protected niches. As a primary agent of globalization, multinational business represents for many a challenge and a threat. That fact, coupled with individual mistakes and misjudgments, has put the corporate sector as a whole under intense scrutiny.

Business is responding to that scrutiny. Corporate social responsibility has moved beyond philanthropy to engagement—in helping to solve problems; in offering new and better choices, and engagement, too, through the development of new opportunities—the provision of a ladder for individual and collective progress. Multinational business relies for its success on the health of the global society of which it is part. We can only trade and thrive if there are open flows of knowledge and capital.

In the face of scepticism and scrutiny we have to demonstrate that our activity and presence bring the possibility of progress for everyone. In practical terms that means finding ways to reduce emissions and to demonstrate that it is possible to avert the risks of climate change without destroying the world's economic prospects. It means adopting simple, effective measures of transparency to ensure that the flow of funds generated by our activity can be traced. And it means offering employment and individual development on the basis of merit, embracing diversity and cultural difference—and in doing so lifting the aspirations of the communities of which we are part.

Maps provide a synthesis of what we know. But they do something more. Stephen Hall in the introduction to his book *Mapping the Next Millennium* quotes Primo Levi, who believed that "maps most of all speak the language of possibilities." In the words of Levi's poem, "The First Atlas", "Not one of the lands written into your destiny will speak to you

the language of your first atlas." Great maps show us the areas we do not know—the unexplored territory or what the original mapmakers called "*terra nullius*."

There is other territory to be explored as well. In each of the corporate maps shown here there are large gaps. Multinational business, even after two decades of rapid growth, probably still reaches less than half the world's population. Globalization is still a very partial phenomenon, and many still lack the means or the freedom to enjoy the choices we take for granted. For those of us who believe passionately that globalization is a good thing that represents the next frontier—the map still to be drawn.

I congratulate the authors on the fascinating book they have produced, and I look forward to the publication of each successive edition.

John Browne, CEO, BP
2003

# Acknowledgments

The authors would like to thank and acknowledge the distinguished Advisory Board of the Mapping the Multinational Corporations Project.

## ADVISORY BOARD

**Alfred Chandler** is the Isidor Straus Professor of Business History, Emeritus, at the Harvard Business School, and winner of both the Bancroft Prize and the Pulitzer Prize in History for *The Visible Hand: The Managerial Revolution in American Business*. He is also the author of *Strategy and Structure: Chapters in the History of the American Industrial Enterprise* and *Scale and Scope: The Dynamics of Industrial Capitalism*.

**John H. Dunning** is State of New Jersey Professor of International Business at Rutgers University, USA, and professor emeritus in international business at the University of Reading, UK. Among other works, he is the author of the textbook *Multinational Enterprises and the Global Economy* and editor of *Governments, Globalization, and International Business*.

**Neva Goodwin** is a codirector of the Global Development and Environment Institute at Tufts University. She is supervising the six-volume project *Frontier Issues in Economic Thought* and is editing four books under the series title *Evolving Values for a Capitalist World*. Dr. Goodwin's latest project is the development of an introductory economics textbook, *Microeconomics in Context*.

**Geoffrey Jones** is a former professor of business history at the Centre for International Business History at the University of Reading, UK, and is now at the Harvard Business School. He is a former president of the Association of Business Historians in the UK, and is currently secretary-treasurer of the European Business History Association. Among his publications are *The Multinational Traders* (ed.), *British Multinationals: Origins, Management, and Performance*, and *The Evolution of International Business*.

**Stephen J. Kobrin** is the William H. Wurster Professor of Multinational Management and director of the Joseph H. Lauder Institute of Management and International Studies and the William H. Wurster Center for International Management Studies at the Wharton Business School of the University of Pennsylvania. His publications include *What Is a Global Firm?* and *Beyond Geography: Interfirm Networks and the Structural Integration of the Global Economy*.

**Bruce Mazlish** is a professor of history at the Massachusetts Institute of Technology, and a fellow of the American Academy of Arts and Sciences. In 1986 he was awarded the Toynbee Prize. He has spearheaded an effort to conceptualize global history (editing a volume titled *Conceptualizing Global History*, with Ralph Buultjens, which appeared in 1993). His most recent publications are *The Uncertain Sciences* and *The Fourth Discontinuity: The Co-evolution of Humans and Machines*.

**Robert A. G. Monks** is a cofounder of Lens, an activist investment management firm based on shareholder rights. He was an official in the U.S. Labor Department. His published works include *Power and Accountability* and *Watching the Watchers*.

**Elliott Morss** is a principal of the Asia-Pacific Group investment firm and treasurer of the Toynbee Prize Foundation.

**Mira Wilkins** is a professor of economics at Florida International University. She is the author of two standard histories of American multinational business, *The Emergence of Multinational Enterprise: American Business Abroad from the Colonial Era to 1914* and *Maturing of Multinational Enterprise*.

The authors would like to single out for special thanks Bruce Mazlish, Alfred Chandler, Stephen Kobrin, and Mira Wilkins for their extra efforts with various sections of the book. This effort was sponsored by the Ford Foundation under Grant No. 980-1089/1005. The views and conclusions contained herein are those of the authors and should not be interpreted as necessarily representing the official policies or endorsements, either expressed or implied, of the Rockefeller Brothers Foundation or the Ford Foundation.

## RESEARCH ASSISTANTS

Clarissa Fesler
University of Pennsylvania
Economics, International Relations

Tara Hanson
Bryn Mawr College
Economics

Daniel Matisoff
University of Pennsylvania
Economics, International Relations

Rupa Raman
Wharton School
University of Pennsylvania
Economics, Finance, and Global Analysis

Robert Rutkin
University of Pennsylvania
Economics, International Relations

Clara Teo
University of Pennsylvania
Economics, Urban Studies

Jennifer Yau
Wharton School
University of Pennsylvania
Public Policy and Management

## GRAPHIC DESIGN/WEB DEVELOPMENT

Ricardo Eric Gálvez
University of the Arts, Philadelphia

# Introduction

The geography of nations is easy to see. Spin a globe and put your finger down anywhere on a landmass and there will be a country. The nation is a geographically fixed organization. Its borders, like most of its decisions, are relatively slow-moving. The "mass" and "momentum" of the nation-state keep it moving, but most change happens slowly.

The geography of multinational corporations is not so easy to perceive. They are not as "big"; that is, their geographic footprint does not take up as much room. Corporations exist more in the marketplace than they do in geographic space, and it is from their presence in the marketplace that their size and power originates.

The rapid rise over the last few decades in the size, number, and influence of multinational corporations has garnered a great deal of international attention from governments, nongovernmental organizations (NGOs), the media, and concerned citizens from all walks of life. Much of this concern stems from the fact that many modern multinational corporations have developed resources to such an extent that they are no longer answerable to any national government. In the past, government regulation was the fundamental method of governance and oversight of big business, providing a check against corporations running roughshod over the public interest.

These days, however, corporations are more nimble than their country cousins. "With their vast resources and technical capabilities they can invent and implement solutions faster than government agencies, perhaps faster than we can imagine."[1] Without the responsibilities of nationhood, the corporation can move quickly when challenge or opportunity strikes. When unfettered by national or international laws, ecological understanding, or social responsibility, this freedom can lead to enormously destructive acts. At the same time, their agility, initiative, focused power, and access to capital and resources allow them to innovate, create, produce goods and services, and influence the world on a scale and at a speed far beyond those of a nation-state and at a rate the world has never seen before.

However one perceives the phenomenon of the multinational corporation, an objective look at what they are is essential for successful navigation into the 21st century. We need to understand their history, what brought them into being and nurtures their continuing growth. *Global Inc.* attempts to do this. It seeks to answer such fundamental questions regarding multinational corporations as: Who are they? Where did they come from? How did they evolve? and What do they do? In addition, it seeks spatially to answer these questions through visual representations of the historical and economic geography of multinational corporations, both as a group and with a focus on notable examples.

Chapter 1 establishes the context and rationale for examining multinational corporations. Important facts regarding the number, size, extent, and impact of multinational corporate activity are presented.

Chapter 2 is a summary of the factors that brought the multinational corporation into being. Globalization and how it allowed the modern corporation to become a global phenomenon with unprecedented power is illustrated through text, charts, graphs, and maps. This chapter sets the scene for the global corporation by explaining the forces, dynamics, and history of globalization and its impact on the economy, technology, culture, government, corporations, and environment.

Chapter 3 illustrates the predecessors and history of modern multinational corporations. The origins of international trade are traced back to early trading routes and growing connections among the regional economies of Europe and North Africa, the Far East, Latin America, and sub-Saharan Africa. Then the ancestors of multinational business, European trading and banking organizations of the Middle Ages, are presented. In the 1600s the era of "Global Trading Companies" begins. The English East India Company, the Dutch East India Company, the Hudson's Bay Company, and other international limited-liability companies of the era are mapped and described. Next, the patterns of international investment by multinational corporations that outline the "first" global economy before World War I are depicted. Finally, through maps and charts of foreign investment, mergers and acquisitions, and multinational corporate headquarters, the evolution of multinational business from 1914 to 2001 is presented.

Chapter 4 introduces contemporary global corporations. Twenty-five corporations, from 17 different sectors of the global economy (e.g., petroleum, computers, telecommunications, food, and media and entertainment), are mapped in detail as models of the phenomenon of the global corporation. Each section begins with an iconic map of the world's largest corporations from one sector, accompanied by key facts and figures. Then representative and notable corporations, such as General Motors, Toyota, IBM, AT&T, Microsoft, British Petroleum, and AOL Time Warner are mapped in detail. Employment, growth and geographical spread through time, sales and revenue, production, and office locations are among the items presented.

Chapter 5 illustrates the worldwide economic, environmental, social, and cultural impacts of multinational corporations through maps, charts, and text. Throughout *Global Inc.* a balanced accounting is sought, not simply an anecdotal litany of corporate wrongdoings or virtues.

Chapter 6 presents a discussion of corporate governance, control, and accountability as well as some of the incentives that the nation-state, city, and community have for encouraging the most constructive aspects of the global corporation and discouraging or avoiding the negative qualities.

The book does not pretend or intend to be definitive. It maps a small fraction of the more than 63,000 multinational corporations and their impacts on the world. What we sought to do in this first atlas of the global corporation was to achieve as wide a breadth of coverage as possible, conveying the scope and scale of the global corporation. In a sense, we perceived our task as analogous to early cartographers who sought to create a map of the whole world, to place the continents in the right places and show how they all fit together as a whole system. The intricate details and nuances of each coastline, reef, and harbor depth were left for later explorers and cartographers to fill in. It is our hope that we and others will soon begin these further explorations, and that subsequent editions of *Global Inc.* will provide the world with better and sharper maps of the world of multinational corporations.

Global Inc.

# I. Global Inc.

*Since the middle of the 17th century, the state has been the most important...of all modern institutions. It is now in decline, either voluntarily or involuntarily.*
—Martin van Crevell, *The Rise and Decline of the State*

*While some regard them as ruthless exploiters, others view them as benign engines of prosperity. But today's multinationals bear little resemblance to their forebearers. They are reinventing themselves in diverse ways that confound the assumptions of critics and advocates alike.*
—John Stopford, "Multinational Corporations," *Foreign Policy*

The modern nation-state and corporation both had their beginnings around the same time. The Treaty of Westphalia in 1648 is often cited as the point from which the modern nation-state originated, and the public charter that created the first joint stock company in England was put in place by Elizabeth I in 1600. From these origins, both forms of organization have grown in number, geographical extent, and power. From a few nations to more than 220 in the year 2001, and from a handful of corporations to more than 63,000 multinational corporations, both now envelop the world.

Of these two, the nation-state has historically been the most important and powerful. This is changing. Corporations, specifically multinational corporations, are gaining power relative to the nation. This new power arrangement is not merely the result of the nation-state giving up existing powers, although that is happening. More important, new power is being brought into the world in the form of new technology that the multinational corporations have control over, and it is this new technology that is expanding the power and prerogatives of the multinational corporation. Additionally, because they are quicker and more agile than their national counterparts, corporations can more readily leverage the forces of globalization.

Given the new balances of power arising from the complex interactions of the multinational corporation and nation-state, it is imperative that we look closely at what is happening:

- **Multinational corporations are big—and they are getting bigger.** In terms of corporate revenue versus the gross domestic product (GDP) of countries, of the 100 largest economies in the world, 53 are corporations.[1] ExxonMobil, the largest corporation in the world, is larger than more than 180 nations.

- **There are a lot of multinational corporations—and their numbers are growing fast.** There were around 3,000 in 1900. By 1970 there were close to 7,000, and by 1990 the number had swelled to an incredible 30,000. A decade later there were more than 63,000.[2]

## The World's 100 Largest Economies
Corporate Revenue vs. Country GDP 2000 (millions US$)

| # | Name | Value | # | Name | Value |
|---|------|-------|---|------|-------|
| 1 | United States | $9,882,842 | 51 | Iran | $98,991 |
| 2 | Japan | $4,677,099 | 52 | Egypt | $98,333 |
| 3 | Germany | $1,870,136 | 53 | Ireland | $94,388 |
| 4 | United Kingdom | $1,413,432 | 54 | Axa | $92,781 |
| 5 | France | $1,286,252 | 55 | Singapore | $92,252 |
| 6 | China | $1,079,954 | 56 | Sumitomo | $91,168 |
| 7 | Italy | $1,068,518 | 57 | Malaysia | $89,321 |
| 8 | Canada | $689,550 | 58 | IBM | $88,396 |
| 9 | Brazil | $587,553 | 59 | Marunbeni | $85,351 |
| 10 | Mexico | $574,512 | 60 | Colombia | $82,849 |
| 11 | Spain | $555,004 | 61 | Volkswagen | $78,851 |
| 12 | India | $479,404 | 62 | Hitachi | $76,126 |
| 13 | Korea, Rep. | $457,219 | 63 | Philippines | $75,186 |
| 14 | Australia | $394,023 | 64 | Siemens | $74,858 |
| 15 | Netherlands | $364,948 | 65 | ING Group | $71,195 |
| 16 | Argentina | $285,473 | 66 | Allianz | $71,022 |
| 17 | Russian Federation | $251,092 | 67 | Chile | $70,710 |
| 18 | Switzerland | $240,323 | 68 | Matsushita | $69,475 |
| 19 | Belgium | $231,016 | 69 | E.on | $68,432 |
| 20 | Sweden | $227,369 | 70 | Nippon Life Insurance | $68,054 |
| 21 | ExxonMobil | $210,392 | 71 | Deutsche Bank | $67,133 |
| 22 | Turkey | $199,902 | 72 | Sony | $66,158 |
| 23 | Wal-Mart | $193,295 | 73 | AT&T | $65,981 |
| 24 | Austria | $190,957 | 74 | Verizon | $64,707 |
| 25 | General Motors | $184,632 | 75 | U.S. Postal Service | $64,540 |
| 26 | Ford | $180,598 | 76 | Philip Morris | $63,276 |
| 27 | Hong Kong | $163,261 | 77 | Pakistan | $61,673 |
| 28 | Denmark | $160,780 | 78 | CGNU | $61,498 |
| 29 | Poland | $158,839 | 79 | J. P. Morgan & Chase | $60,065 |
| 30 | Indonesia | $153,255 | 80 | Carrefour | $59,887 |
| 31 | DaimlerChrysler | $150,069 | 81 | Credit Suisse | $59,315 |
| 32 | Norway | $149,349 | 82 | Nissho Iwai | $58,557 |
| 33 | Royal Dutch/Shell | $149,146 | 83 | Honda | $58,461 |
| 34 | BP | $148,062 | 84 | Bank of America | $57,747 |
| 35 | General Electric | $129,853 | 85 | BNP Paribas | $57,611 |
| 36 | Mitsubishi | $126,579 | 86 | Nissan | $55,077 |
| 37 | South Africa | $125,887 | 87 | Peru | $53,882 |
| 38 | Thailand | $121,927 | 88 | Toshiba | $53,826 |
| 39 | Toyota | $121,416 | 89 | Algeria | $53,817 |
| 40 | Venezuela | $120,484 | 90 | PDVSA | $53,680 |
| 41 | Finland | $119,823 | 91 | Assicurazione Generali | $53,333 |
| 42 | Mitsui | $118,013 | 92 | Fiat | $53,190 |
| 43 | Greece | $111,955 | 93 | Mizuho | $52,068 |
| 44 | Citigroup | $111,826 | 94 | SBC Communications | $51,476 |
| 45 | Israel | $110,332 | 95 | Boeing | $51,321 |
| 46 | Itochu | $109,756 | 96 | Texaco | $51,130 |
| 47 | Total FINA Elf | $105,869 | 97 | New Zealand | $49,983 |
| 48 | Portugal | $103,871 | 98 | Fujitsu | $49,603 |
| 49 | NTT | $103,234 | 99 | Czech Republic | $49,510 |
| 50 | Enron | $100,789 | 100 | Duke Energy | $49,318 |

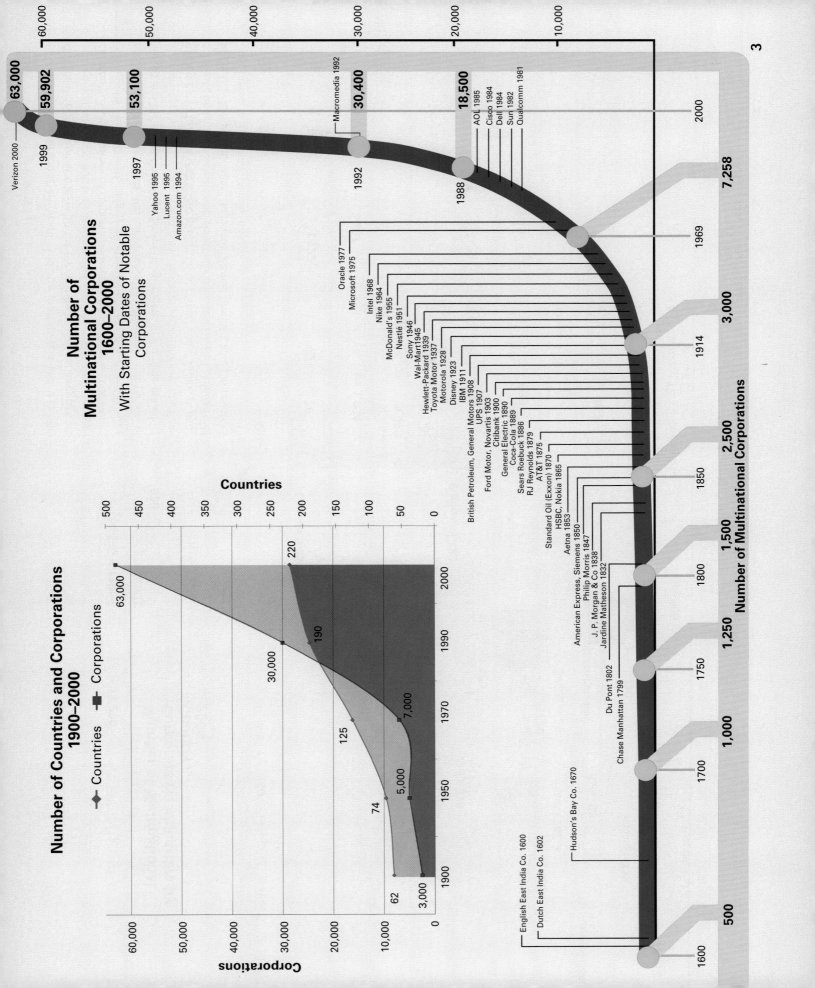

# Number of Multinational Corporations 1600-2000

With Starting Dates of Notable Corporations

## Number of Countries and Corporations 1900-2000

Countries

- ◆ Countries
- ■ Corporations

Corporations scale: 0; 10,000; 20,000; 30,000; 40,000; 50,000; 60,000

Countries scale: 0; 50; 100; 150; 200; 250; 300; 350; 400; 450; 500

Years: 1900, 1950, 1970, 1990, 2000

Data points:
- 63,000
- 30,000
- 7,000
- 5,000
- 3,000
- 220
- 190
- 125
- 74
- 62

**Number of Multinational Corporations**

63,000 — Verizon 2000
59,902 — 1999
53,100 — 1997
30,400 — Macromedia 1992 / 1992
18,500 — 1988

Yahoo 1995
Lucent 1995
Amazon.com 1994

AOL 1985
Cisco 1984
Dell 1984
Sun 1982
Qualcomm 1981

7,258 — 1969

Oracle 1977
Microsoft 1975
Intel 1968
Nike 1964
McDonald's 1955
Nestlé 1951
Sony 1946
Wal-Mart 1945
Hewlett-Packard 1939
Toyota Motor 1937
Motorola 1928
Disney 1923
IBM 1911
British Petroleum, General Motors 1908
UPS 1907
Ford Motor, Novartis 1903
Citibank 1900
General Electric 1890
Coca-Cola 1889
Sears Roebuck 1886
RJ Reynolds 1879
AT&T 1875
Standard Oil (Exxon) 1870
HSBC, Nokia 1865
Aetna 1853
American Express, Siemens 1850
Philip Morris 1847
J. P. Morgan & Co 1838
Jardine Matheson 1832

3,000 — 1914
1,850 — 1850
1,800 — 1800

Du Pont 1802
Chase Manhattan 1799

1,750 — 1750
1,000 — 1700
1,700

Hudson's Bay Co. 1670

700 — 1700

English East India Co. 1600
Dutch East India Co. 1602

500 — 1600

Number of Multinational Corporations scale: 500; 1,000; 1,250; 1,500; 2,500; 3,000; 7,258

3

• **Global corporations are small—and size matters less and less.** This statement seems to be at odds with the previous point that corporations are big and getting bigger, but both are true. The complex global economy supports both manifestations of corporate enterprise. Most of the 63,000+ firms that operate internationally employ fewer than 250 people, and many service companies have fewer than 100 employees.[3] The economic integration of Europe and the dissolution of the Soviet Union engendered a huge growth in the number of small European firms doing business across borders; tiny Denmark is home to more than 9,000 multinational corporations.[4] Although huge corporations, which dominate the global economy, tend to be headquartered in the U.S., Europe, and Japan, thousands of small firms are based in countries from Tunisia to Bulgaria, Oman to Guyana.

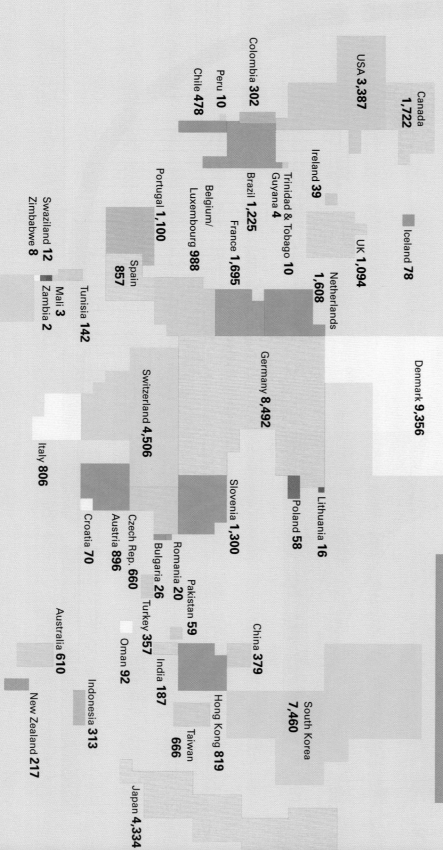

## Number of Multinational Corporate Headquarters by Country 2000

☐ = 1,000 Company Headquarters
▫ = 100 Company Headquarters

Canada **1,722**

USA **3,387**

Colombia **302**

Peru **10**

Chile **478**

Iceland **78**

Ireland **39**

UK **1,094**

Netherlands **1,608**

Trinidad & Tobago **10**

Guyana **4**

Brazil **1,225**

France **1,695**

Belgium/ Luxembourg **988**

Portugal **1,100**

Spain **857**

Tunisia **142**

Swaziland **12**

Zimbabwe **8**

Mali **3**

Zambia **2**

South Africa **941**

Switzerland **4,506**

Italy **806**

Germany **8,492**

Slovenia **1,300**

Poland **58**

Lithuania **16**

Denmark **9,356**

Norway **900**

Sweden **5,118**

Finland **1,200**

Croatia **70**

Czech Rep. **660**

Austria **896**

Bulgaria **26**

Romania **20**

Turkey **357**

Oman **92**

Pakistan **59**

China **379**

India **187**

Hong Kong **819**

Taiwan **666**

South Korea **7,460**

Japan **4,334**

Australia **610**

Indonesia **313**

New Zealand **217**

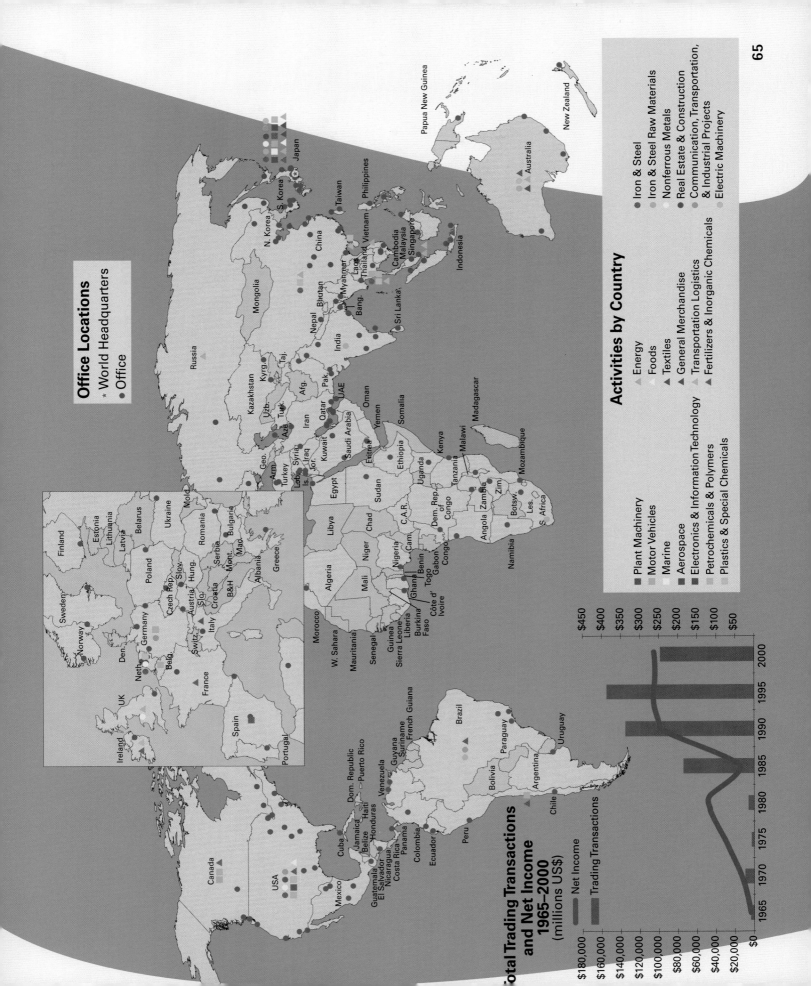

**Office Locations**
★ World Headquarters
● Office

**Activities by Country**

| Plant Machinery | ▲ Energy | ● Iron & Steel |
|---|---|---|
| Motor Vehicles | ▲ Foods | ● Iron & Steel Raw Materials |
| Marine | ▲ Textiles | ● Nonferrous Metals |
| Aerospace | ▲ General Merchandise | ● Real Estate & Construction |
| Electronics & Information Technology | ▲ Transportation Logistics | ● Communication, Transportation, & Industrial Projects |
| Petrochemicals & Polymers | ▲ Fertilizers & Inorganic Chemicals | ● Electric Machinery |
| Plastics & Special Chemicals | | |

**Total Trading Transactions and Net Income 1965–2000** (millions US$)

— Net Income
▬ Trading Transactions

$180,000
$160,000
$140,000
$120,000
$100,000
$80,000
$60,000
$40,000
$20,000
$0

$450
$400
$350
$300
$250
$200
$150
$100
$50

1965 1970 1975 1980 1985 1990 1995 2000

# Computers and Electronics

- 25 years ago only **50,000** computers existed; today there are an estimated **600 million or more.** By 2007 there will be approximately **1.15 billion.**

- In 1985 **50%** of the world's computer hardware was produced in the U.S., and **23%** in Asia. Today these proportions are reversed.

- It costs more than **$1 billion** to develop a new computer chip; chip fabrication plants cost **$1 billion to $2 billion** each.

- Global sales in computers and related industries reached **$500 billion** by the late 1990s.

- Worldwide sales of semiconductors are projected to grow from **$149 billion** in 1999 to **$283 billion** by 2004.

- The largest producers of computers in terms of 2000 sales were:

  IBM **$88.3 billion**

  Hitachi **$76.1 billion**

  Siemens **$74.8 billion**

  Matsushita **$69.4 billion**

  Sony **$66.1 billion**

  Toshiba **$53.8 billion**

- Worldwide sales of consumer electronics will top **$95.7 billion** in 2002.

- The number of different consumer electronics products expected to come to market in the next **5 years** will exceed the number introduced over the last **3 decades.**

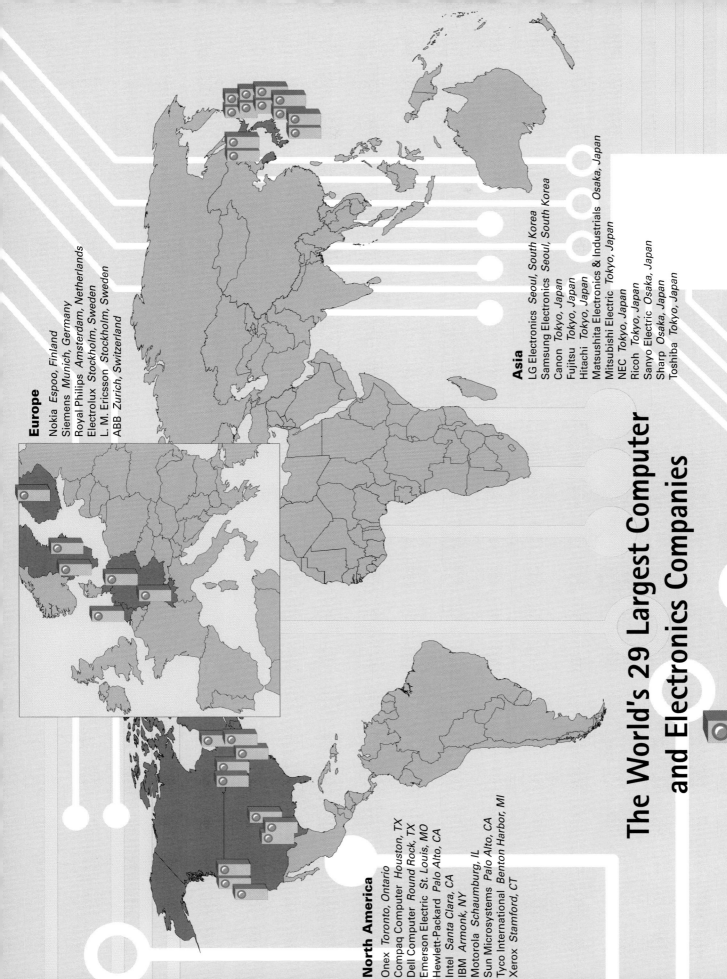

# The World's 29 Largest Computer and Electronics Companies

**North America**

Onex  *Toronto, Ontario*
Compaq Computer  *Houston, TX*
Dell Computer  *Round Rock, TX*
Emerson Electric  *St. Louis, MO*
Hewlett-Packard  *Palo Alto, CA*
Intel  *Santa Clara, CA*
IBM  *Armonk, NY*
Motorola  *Schaumburg, IL*
Sun Microsystems  *Palo Alto, CA*
Tyco International  *Benton Harbor, MI*
Xerox  *Stamford, CT*

**Europe**

Nokia  *Espoo, Finland*
Siemens  *Munich, Germany*
Royal Philips  *Amsterdam, Netherlands*
Electrolux  *Stockholm, Sweden*
L. M. Ericsson  *Stockholm, Sweden*
ABB  *Zurich, Switzerland*

**Asia**

LG Electronics  *Seoul, South Korea*
Samsung Electronics  *Seoul, South Korea*
Canon  *Tokyo, Japan*
Fujitsu  *Tokyo, Japan*
Hitachi  *Tokyo, Japan*
Matsushita Electronics & Industrials  *Osaka, Japan*
Mitsubishi Electric  *Tokyo, Japan*
NEC  *Tokyo, Japan*
Ricoh  *Tokyo, Japan*
Sanyo Electric  *Osaka, Japan*
Sharp  *Osaka, Japan*
Toshiba  *Tokyo, Japan*

= Corporate Headquarters

# IBM

Charles Ranlett Flint founded the Calculating-Tabulating-Recording (CTR) Company in 1910 as an alliance of a clock/time-device company, a scales and measures company, and a company that specialized in machines that tabulated punched cards. CTR's tabulating machine was used for the U.S. Census in 1880 and 1900, and was soon in demand by other organizations encountering the newly emerging need to manipulate large amounts of information. In 1924 CTR changed its name to International Business Machines (IBM) and began to focus solely on the technology service industry.

The highly profitable company grew rapidly throughout the 1910s and 1920s. In 1932 IBM faced what would be a long series of antitrust suits. A 1952 suit by the Justice Department, settled four years later, forced IBM to sell its tabulating machines instead of just leasing them as had been its practice, and to discontinue a number of card-producing facilities. Competing companies filed 20 antitrust actions during the 1970s, none of which succeeded.

New markets for IBM's calculating machines kept appearing. After the depression, the New Deal created a vast federal bureaucracy that demanded accounting machines and keypunchers. The new Social Security Administration placed huge orders for tabulating equipment. During World War II machines were needed to monitor the manufacture and the movement of the war effort's enormous resources. In addition, IBM created high-speed calculators for the military in order to solve ballistics equations and to help with the development of the atomic bomb. IBM also joined the partnership that was building the new Electronic Numerical Integrator and Calculator (ENIAC) at the University of Pennsylvania, the world's first all-electronic computer.

Initially IBM was cautious about entering the nascent computer market, but a huge research push by the company in the early 1950s put IBM into the lead in the computer industry by 1956. The 85% of offices using IBM tabulating machines easily switched to using IBM computers. By 1949, IBM operated in 58 countries, but the volume of overseas business was small. A new IBM World Trade subsidiary began to focus on the market overseas, and foreign IBM units often monopolized local markets. During the 1960s IBM installed more than 90% of the computers in Europe; today 60% of IBM's sales are overseas.

Although IBM tended to be behind the curve in technological innovation, the company completely dominated the market for computers from 1960 into the 1980s, and also developed other commercially successful technologies such as barcode scanners and early automatic teller machines. However, after a peak in 1984, the rapidly increasing pace of technological change began to leave "Big Blue" behind. IBM market share dropped, and the firm was no longer the juggernaut it had once been. The market for mainframe computers had shrunk as computers had become smaller and applied to a broader range of tasks. By 1993 IBM's annual net losses reached a staggering $8 billion.

IBM responded to the new, faster technology markets by reorganizing into a holding company with independently functioning branches, each of which can function faster and more competitively. Recent years have brought more success to IBM, as the company narrowed its focus on the world of network computing and e-commerce, returning to its roots by providing ongoing technological services to corporations. From 1993 to 1996, the market value of the company increased by more than $50 billion.

IBM is also an important presence in researching new technologies. In a demonstration of the company's progress in supercomputing, in 1997 the IBM computer "Deep Blue" defeated world chess champion Garry Kasparov. It was the first time a computer had beaten a top-ranked chess player in tournament play. IBM also pursues practical and exploratory research in materials, nanotechnology, supercomputing, networking, and other high-tech fields.

Today IBM is the world's largest provider of computer hardware and services, and the world's second largest software developer (behind Microsoft). The company's 2000 total revenues topped $88 billion.

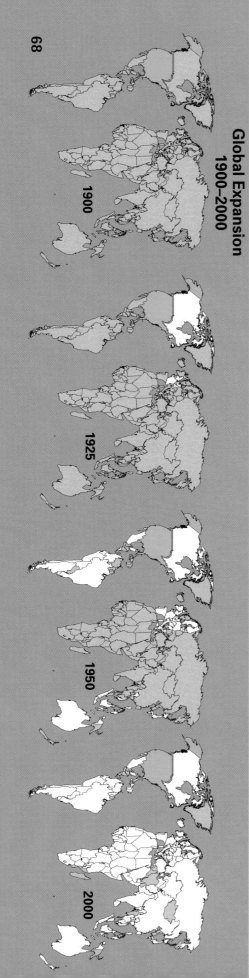

**Global Expansion
1900–2000**

1900

1925

1950

2000

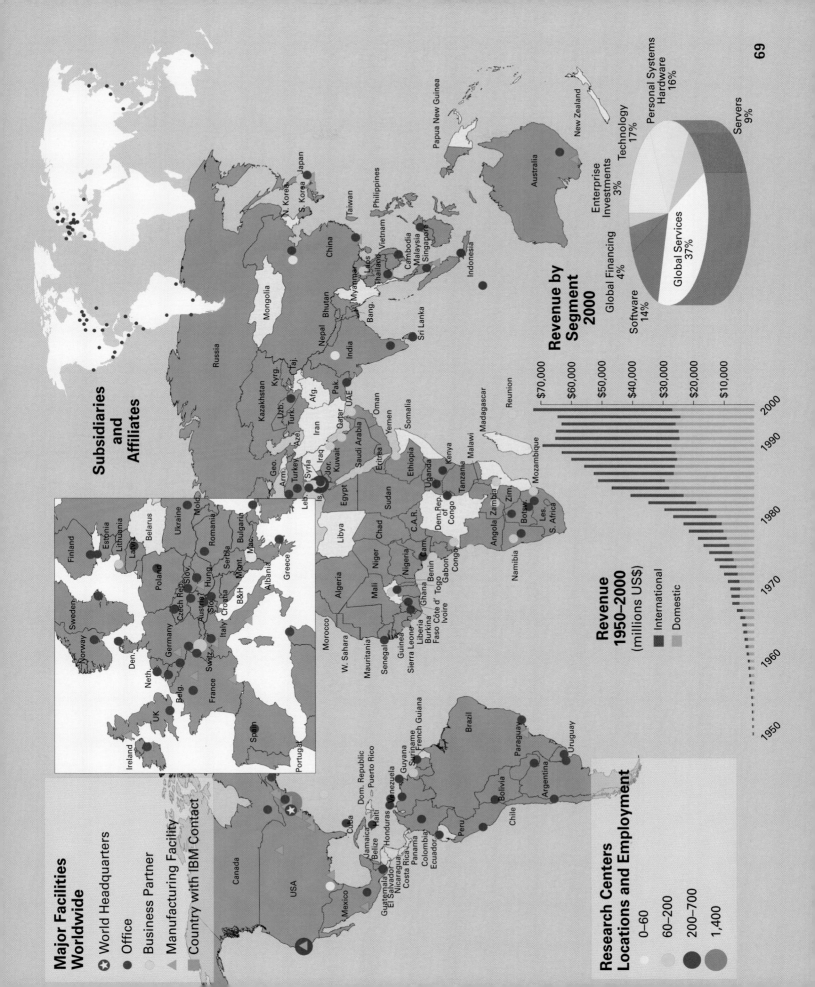

**Major Facilities Worldwide**

- ★ World Headquarters
- ● Office
- ○ Business Partner
- ◤ Manufacturing Facility
- ▪ Country with IBM Contact

**Subsidiaries and Affiliates**

**Revenue by Segment 2000**

- Global Services 37%
- Technology 17%
- Personal Systems 16%
- Hardware
- Software 14%
- Servers 9%
- Global Financing 4%
- Enterprise Investments 3%

**Revenue 1950–2000** (millions US$)

- International
- Domestic

$70,000
$60,000
$50,000
$40,000
$30,000
$20,000
$10,000

1950  1960  1970  1980  1990  2000

**Research Centers Locations and Employment**

- ○ 0–60
- ● 60–200
- ● 200–700
- ● 1,400

69

# Siemens

The origins of Siemens date back to 1847, when Werner Siemens developed an improved telegraph and formed the Siemens & Halske Telegraph Construction Company in Berlin with partner Johann Halske. The firm laid the first long-distance telegraph line in Europe only a year later, connecting the cities of Berlin and Frankfurt. Siemens & Halske continued telegraph construction throughout Europe, extending its network to Russia and England.

As the firm continued to expand its international presence, its telegraph operations assumed a grander scale. In 1870 and 1871 Siemens linked London to Calcutta and Tehran by telegraph. Only five years later Siemens Brothers, the firm's British affiliate, laid the first transatlantic cable between Ireland and the United States. By the early 1900s, Siemens was involved in power generation, the nascent Xray technology, electrified railways, and elevators.

The history of Siemens AG in the first half of the 20th century reflects the tumult of the period, as the company's fortunes rose and fell with the German states. During World War I, Siemens produced communications equipment, explosives, airplane engines, and fire-control systems for the military. The company suffered badly with Germany's defeat, and its important Russian and British subsidiaries were both nationalized.

The firm recovered during the 1920s and expanded into the newly industrializing Japanese market. The Great Depression hurt Siemens terribly, until the German rearmament leading up to World War II began generating business. By 1940 all of Siemens's capacity was directed toward military production; in 1944 Siemens helped develop the V-2 rocket. The company was devastated by Germany's loss and by allegations of the use of slave labor and of supplying death camps with gas chamber equipment.

The company recovered quickly after the war. Siemens engineering played a role in the transmission by the American Mars probe *Mariner 4* of photographs back to Earth in 1965. By 1970, Siemens was involved in electron microscopes, high-speed trains, nuclear power, computers, and space probes. By the late 1970s, Siemens's research and development budget of $1 billion equaled an eighth of all West German research, and Siemens set out to take on Silicon Valley in developing microchips. The smaller Silicon Valley companies prevailed, and Siemens met with a huge loss on the project. From 1983 to 1988 Siemens spent $24 billion on research and acquisitions in a long-term bid to become a global leader in high tech.

The company charged into the globalized 1990s, pursuing markets in Asia and South America and giving local managers greater control. A 1998 alliance between global giants—Siemens, IBM, and Toshiba—to develop a new processor chip was seen as the new wave of the borderless corporate future, where even the largest corporations seek capital, and technological assistance and cooperation, to make the colossal investments necessary for further gains in high technology.

Siemens is now the world's second largest (after Hitachi) electrical and electronics company. The company produces more than 50,000 different products ranging from nuclear power plants to tiny optical switches. Siemens now has more than 400 production facilities in 40 countries, and is represented in practically every country in the world. It has 480,000 employees in more than 190 countries, with 60,000 of them performing research work. Siemens registers an average of 28 patents a day, on everything from the world's fastest telephone switch to medical imaging processes and equipment. A typical large project is computerizing Great Britain's visa and immigrations system.

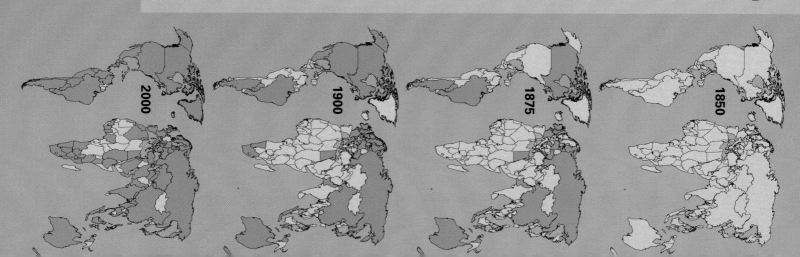

## Global Expansion 1850–2000

1850

1875

1900

2000

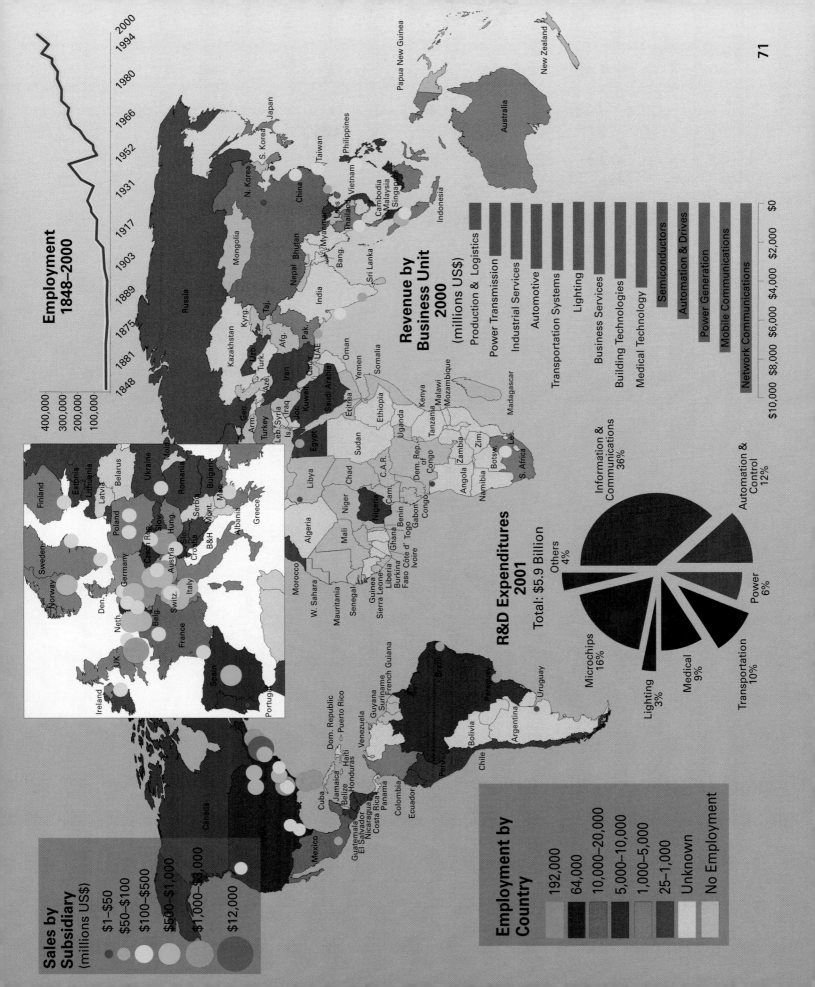

**Sales by Subsidiary**
(millions US$)

- $1–$50
- $50–$100
- $100–$500
- $500–$1,000
- $1,000–$3,000
- $12,000

**Employment 1848–2000**

400,000
300,000
200,000
100,000

2000
1994
1980
1966
1952
1931
1917
1903
1889
1875
1881
1848

**Revenue by Business Unit 2000**
(millions US$)

- Production & Logistics
- Power Transmission
- Industrial Services
- Automotive
- Transportation Systems
- Lighting
- Business Services
- Building Technologies
- Medical Technology
- Semiconductors
- Automation & Drives
- Power Generation
- Mobile Communications
- Network Communications

$10,000  $8,000  $6,000  $4,000  $2,000  $0

**R&D Expenditures 2001**
Total: $5.9 Billion

- Information & Communications 36%
- Automation & Control 12%
- Power 6%
- Transportation 10%
- Medical 9%
- Lighting 3%
- Microchips 16%
- Others 4%

**Employment by Country**

- 192,000
- 64,000
- 10,000–20,000
- 5,000–10,000
- 1,000–5,000
- 25–1,000
- Unknown
- No Employment

71

# LG Electronics

Following the lead of early Japanese exporters of electronics, the founder of the Lucky Goldstar Group, Koo In-Hwoi, created Goldstar in 1958 to make electric appliances. The company led South Korea in innovation in its early years; Goldstar became the first South Korean company to make radios (1959), refrigerators (1965), televisions (1966), elevators and escalators (1968), and washing machines and air conditioners (1969).

Goldstar established new electronics companies through the 1970s and 1980s, and pursued overseas electronics markets. The company exported electronics to JCPenney and Sears that sold as store brands, and also sold radios to Zenith. Growing markets for electronics overseas and inexpensive Korean labor led to LGE's rapid growth. In the late 1970s Goldstar began pursuing high-tech options, investing heavily in semiconductor production. Joint ventures with technically advanced partners AT&T, NEC, Siemens, and Hitachi provided further high-tech resources.

Goldstar founded the company's first overseas subsidiary in the United States in 1978 in order to avoid trade barriers. More international expansion quickly followed, with sales subsidiaries and plants in the U.S. and Europe, and joint ventures in the Philippines, Thailand, the UK, Egypt, Indonesia, and Italy, among others. In 1991, Goldstar purchased a share of Zenith electronics in order to begin to catch up technologically to its Japanese competitors, and in 1994 Goldstar completed the acquisition of Zenith.

In order to continue its reorganization, Goldstar launched the LG label to replace the former Goldstar label for electronics. Along with much of the electronics and appliance industry, the company is concentrating on high-tech, new-concept products, such as huge flat-screen TVs, digital TV, and ultra-fast optical storage and CD recorders.

The company now spans the globe, with operations in 27 countries and a distribution network throughout 150 nations. Seventy-six percent of its sales occur overseas. The company employs more than 25,000 people around the world, and had sales in 2000 of $13 billion. Its global marketing activities include the International LG Cup Soccer Matches in the Middle East, Africa, and Latin America, and the LG Aladdin Park in Karachi, Pakistan, a theme park.

In 2000, LG Electronics (formerly Goldstar Electronics) was one of the largest manufacturers of electronics products in South Korea, and the 15th largest in the world. The company is a member of the LG Group (formerly Lucky-Goldstar), Korea's third largest *chaebol* (industrial group) after Samsung and Hyundai. LG Electronics is the chaebol's lead electronics company. LGE has a global network of branches and plants, and 10 consolidated subsidiaries: six in South Korea, three in the U.S., and one in the UK. Today the company's products range from consumer electronics and home appliances such as TVs, VCRs, refrigerators, and air conditioners, to display devices such as CPTs/CDTs, monitors, and PDPs, to information systems products, including CD-ROMs and PCs.

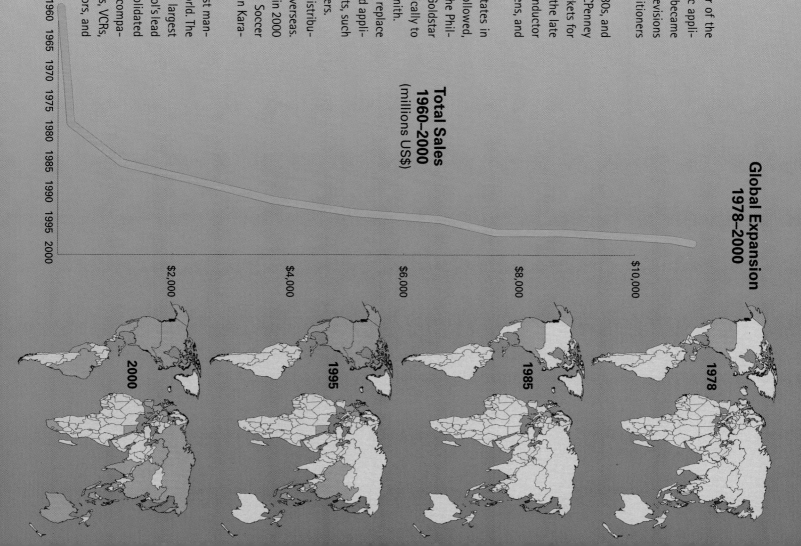

**Global Expansion
1978–2000**

**Total Sales
1960–2000**
(millions US$)

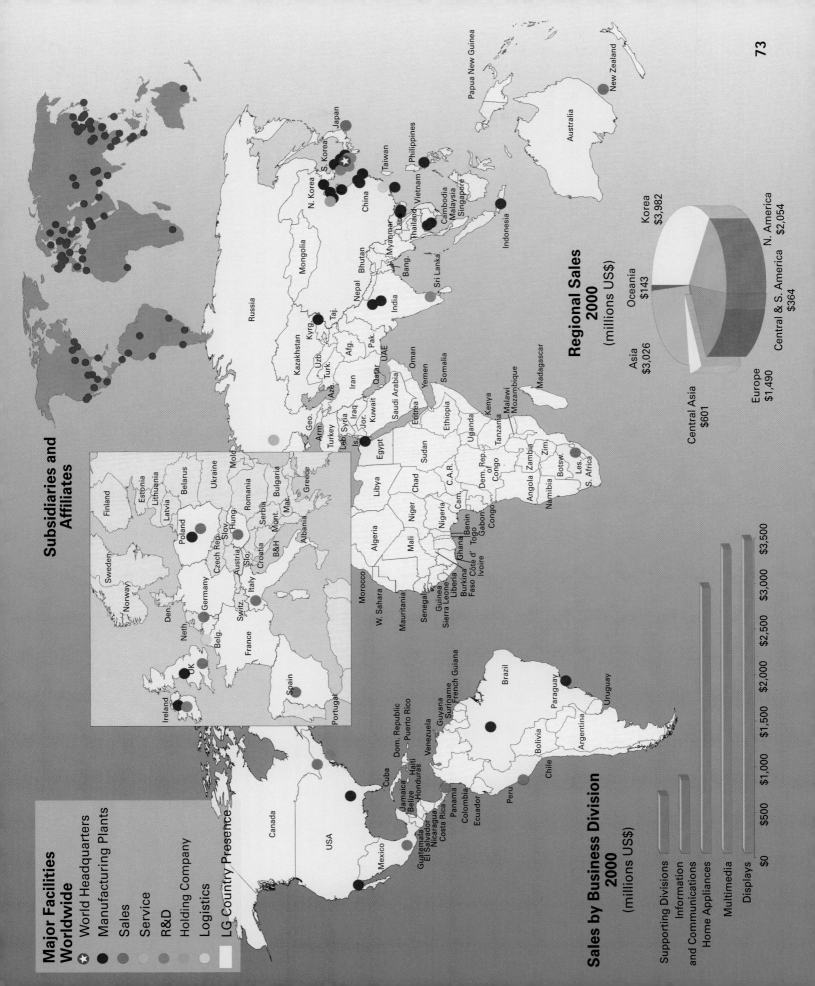

## Subsidiaries and Affiliates

**Major Facilities Worldwide**

- ☆ World Headquarters
- ● Manufacturing Plants
- ● Sales
- ● Service
- ● R&D
- ● Holding Company
- ● Logistics
- ☐ LG Country Presence

### Regional Sales 2000
(millions US$)

- Korea $3,982
- Oceania $143
- Asia $3,026
- Central Asia $601
- Europe $1,490
- Central & S. America $364
- N. America $2,054

### Sales by Business Division 2000
(millions US$)

- Supporting Divisions
- Information and Communications
- Home Appliances
- Multimedia
- Displays

$0    $500    $1,000    $1,500    $2,000    $2,500    $3,000    $3,500

# Software and the Internet

- An estimated 513.4 million people or 8% of the world's population used the Internet in 2001:

  Africa **4.15 million**
  Asia/Pacific **143.99 million**
  Europe **154.63 million**
  Middle East **4.65 million**
  Canada and U.S. **180.68 million**
  Latin America **25.33 million**

- In 2000, there were more than **30 million** Internet domain names.

- Microsoft was the most profitable company in the world in 2000 with a **41%** return on investment.

- It is estimated that in 2002, business-to-consumer on-line transactions will reach **$108 billion;** business-to-business transactions **$1.3 trillion.**

- **100%** of the *Fortune* Global 500 companies now have corporate Web sites, up from **91%** in 1999 and **86%** in 1998.

- **80%** of the *Fortune* Global 500 recruit new staff on their corporate Web sites, up from **60%** in 1999 and **29%** in 1998.

- Worldwide packaged software sales in 2002 are expected to reach **$221.9 billion.**

- Worldwide, **38%** of business software is pirated; **98%** in Vietnam, **95%** in China.

**North America**

Nortel Networks *Brampton, Ontario*
Cisco Systems *San Jose, CA*
Electronic Data Systems *Plano, TX*
Lucent Communications *Murray Hill, NJ*
Microsoft *Redmond, WA*
America Online *Dulles, VA*
JDS Uniphase *San Jose, CA*
Juniper Networks *Sunnyvale, CA*
Broadcom *Irvine, CA*
EMC *Hopkinton, MA*
Ariba *Mountain View, CA*
Network Appliance *Sunnyvale, CA*
Yahoo! *Santa Clara, CA*
Qwest Communications Intl. *Denver, CO*
Exodus Communications *Santa Clara, CA*
Intuit *Mountain View, CA*
CNet Networks *San Francisco, CA*
Oracle *Redwood City, CA*
Computer Associates International *Islandia, NY*
Novell *Provo, UT*
Sybase *Emeryville, CA*
Adobe Systems *San Jose, CA*
Informix *Menlo Park, CA*
American Management Systems *Fairfax, VA*
Compuware *Farmington Hills, MI*
SAS Institute *Cary, NC*
Software AG *Reston, VA*

# The World's 28 Largest Software and Internet Companies

**Europe**

*SAP AG  Walldorf, Germany*

= Corporate Headquarters

# Microsoft

Bill Gates and Paul Allen founded Microsoft in 1975. The company's first product was a programming language called Microsoft BASIC, which was followed by a disk-management program called DiskBASIC. Gates licensed the software to computer makers but retained ownership of the programs, a decision that helped shape the future relationship between computer software and hardware makers. As the company grew, it developed several other programming languages targeting Apple, Tandy, and IBM computers. In a move to begin to consolidate the operating-system market, IBM contracted Microsoft to develop the Microsoft Disk Operating System, or MS-DOS, which was released with the IBM personal computer in 1981 and went on to become one of the most important products in computer history. Over the next few years, MS-DOS was licensed to more than 50 microcomputer manufacturers and became Microsoft's primary product.

The company simultaneously began to develop applications such as Microsoft Word. Realizing that Apple's graphical user interface (GUI) was a likely future direction for personal computing, Gates began publishing software for the Macintosh. By the mid-1980s Microsoft was the primary software producer and supplier for Macintosh computers.

The belief that GUIs were the wave of the future motivated Microsoft to begin work on a new operating system called Windows. This challenge proved to be a particularly daunting task because of the lack of uniformity in DOS programs. Microsoft also faced competition from IBM in the race for a GUI to rival Macintosh's. The release of the first version of Windows was tardy, and the program was at first a flop. Version 2.0 was released in 1987; this version appeared very similar to the Macintosh operating system. It was faster and easier to use than its predecessor, and it sold more than a million copies.

The success of Windows prompted Apple to sue Microsoft for copyright infringement in 1988, claiming that Microsoft had copied "the look and feel" of the Macintosh, beginning a continuous series of legal problems concerning Microsoft's hardball tactics. While the lawsuit wore on in court, Microsoft released Windows 3.0 (which quickly sold more than a million copies,

despite complaints over its usability and its weakness in comparison to the current Macintosh operating system).

The early 1990s was a period of severe competition between Microsoft, IBM, and Apple for control of the burgeoning market for software and operating systems. Over the following decade Microsoft would decisively win those struggles in multiple software and operating-system markets, both in the U.S. and abroad.

In the late 1990s a number of countries—most notably the U.S. but also the European Union, Japan, Brazil, and Israel—began taking legal action against Microsoft's perceived anticompetitive practices. Since 1997, Microsoft has been battling a possible court-ordered breakup of the company as charges have been levied in the U.S. regarding a variety of alleged monopoly practices. As of early 2002, the company had not been ordered to break up, but under the conditions of a possible settlement it would face certain constraints on its business practices for five years.

Microsoft is the world's largest provider of computer software, including operating systems and business, personal, Internet, and software development applications. Over the past 15 years, MS Windows has established almost total market dominance for Intel-based PC operating systems; more than 90% of personal computers are run using Windows. In 2000 the company earned revenues of $22.9 billion; 58% of its revenue currently comes from outside the U.S., and it has operations in more than 70 different countries. One-third of Microsoft's 44,000 employees are employed internationally; Japan has the largest subsidiary, with 945 employees. Microsoft has also pursued aggressive horizontal diversification through providing Internet services, WebTV, video game consoles (Xbox), educational and recreational software, books, and training, among other products.

The company's founder and chairman, Bill Gates, is usually considered the richest person in the world, with an estimated net worth in 2002 of more than $68 billion. In addition to the Windows operating system, Microsoft's other software applications are ubiquitous. The Microsoft name is loved, hated, or merely known and tolerated by literally every person who uses a computer.

## Global Expansion 1975–2000

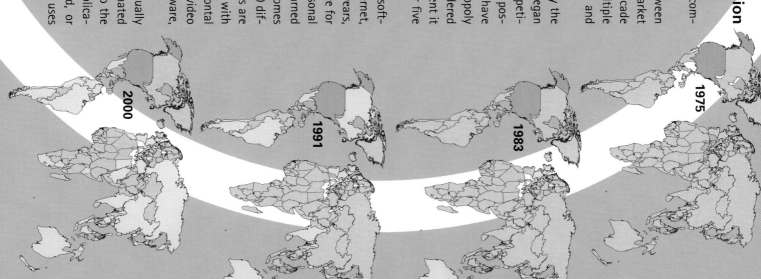

1975

1983

1991

2000

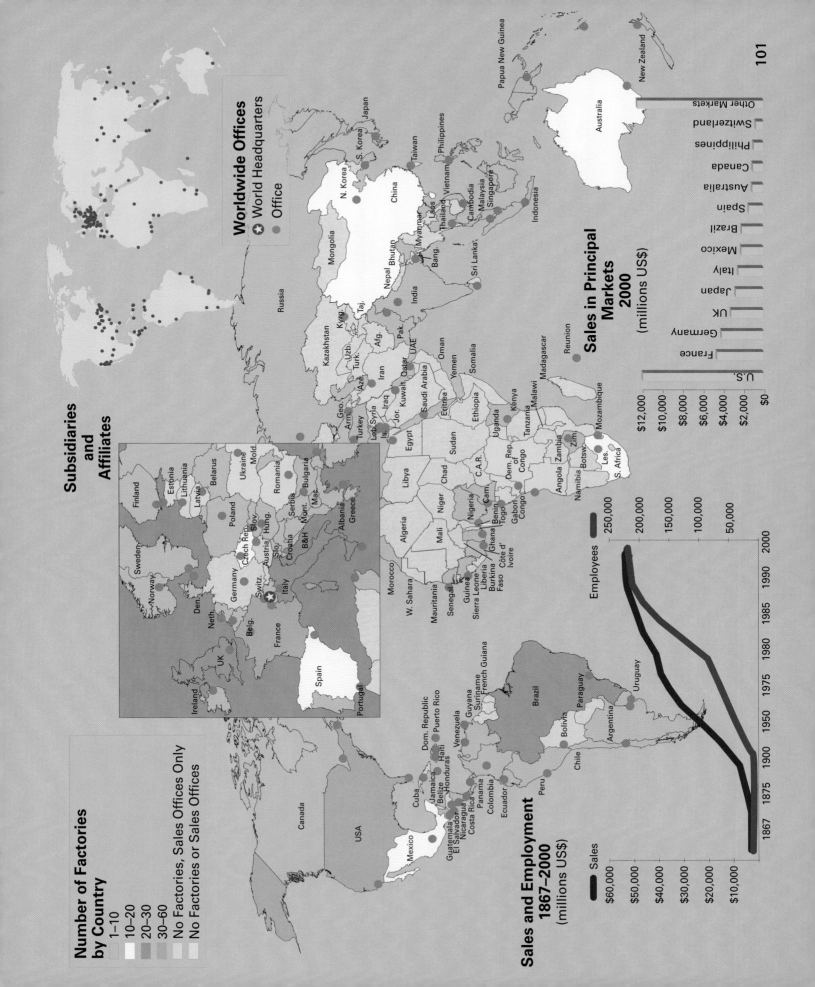

**Number of Factories by Country**
- 1–10
- 10–20
- 20–30
- 30–60
- No Factories, Sales Offices Only
- No Factories or Sales Offices

**Subsidiaries and Affiliates**

**Worldwide Offices**
- ☆ World Headquarters
- ● Office

**Sales in Principal Markets 2000**
(millions US$)

U.S.  France  Germany  UK  Japan  Italy  Mexico  Brazil  Spain  Australia  Canada  Philippines  Switzerland  Other Markets

$12,000  $10,000  $8,000  $6,000  $4,000  $2,000  $0

**Sales and Employment 1867–2000**
(millions US$)

— Sales
— Employees

$60,000  $50,000  $40,000  $30,000  $20,000  $10,000

250,000  200,000  150,000  100,000  50,000

1867  1875  1900  1950  1975  1980  1985  1990  2000

# Advertising

- Worldwide advertising revenues for all media in 2000 was **$243.7 billion.**

- **75%** of the world's advertising is purchased in the U.S., western Europe, and Japan. Most advertising growth in the future will be in Latin America, eastern Europe, China, and the Pacific Rim.

- The world's **3** most recognized brands are McDonald's, Coca-Cola, and Disney.

- The top **10** global advertising organizations account for **33%** of total global ad sales.

- The categories with the most spending on advertising in 1998 were:

  Automotive **$9.9 billion**
  Personal Care **$9.5 billion**
  Food **$5.2 billion**
  Entertainment and Media **$2.4 billion**
  Drugs **$1.5 billion**
  Soft Drinks **$1.3 billion**

- The Marlboro Man was voted the advertising icon of the century by the ad industry.

- **6%** of all advertising revenue will be spent on the Internet by 2005.

# The World's 23 Largest Advertising Firms

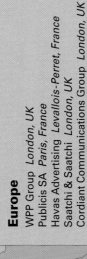

 = Corporate Headquarters

**United States**

Omnicom *New York, NY*
Interpublic Group of Companies *New York, NY*
Bcom3 Group *Chicago, IL*
Young & Rubicam *New York, NY*
Grey Advertising *New York, NY*
True North *Chicago, IL*
TMP Worldwide *New York, NY*
Carlson Marketing Group *Minneapolis, MN*
HA-LO *Niles, IL*
MarchFirst *Chicago, IL*
Aspen Marketing Group *Los Angeles, CA*
Digitas *Boston, MA*
Cyrk/Simon Worldwide *Gloucester, MA*

**Europe**

WPP Group *London, UK*
Publicis SA *Paris, France*
Havas Advertising *Levallois-Perret, France*
Saatchi & Saatchi *London, UK*
Cordiant Communications Group *London, UK*

**Asia**

Dentsu *Tokyo, Japan*
Hakuhodo *Tokyo, Japan*
Asatsu-DK *Tokyo, Japan*
Tokyu Agency *Tokyo, Japan*
Daiko Advertising *Tokyo, Japan*

# Saatchi & Saatchi

Charles and Maurice Saatchi started their advertising agency in London in 1970. Largely by acquiring other ad agencies, within five years Saatchi rose from being the 13th-largest to being the fifth-largest advertising company in the UK. Saatchi & Saatchi continued to buy other advertising firms throughout the 1970s. By buying other firms, Saatchi also acquired the purchased firm's client lists and accounts. It had become the largest advertising company in the UK by 1979, and the largest in Europe two years later.

Saatchi & Saatchi did not grow by acquisitions alone; it also succeeded by its creative advertising work. The company became very well known in the UK for its provocative political campaigns, which were extremely influential in British politics. A famous Saatchi political advertisement targeting the incumbent Labour Party showed a long unemployment line with the tag "Labour Isn't Working." In a campaign for the British Health Education Council's birth-control awareness program, a pregnant man asked, "Would you be more careful if it were you who got pregnant?"

Saatchi & Saatchi is also famous for its hard-nosed business practices. In its goal to become the number-one agency in the world, the company not only does not follow the British advertising trade association's guidelines forbidding the stealing of clients from other firms; it has an entire department that does nothing *but* attempt to steal clients.

In 1986 the company bought the prominent Ted Bates Advertising firm in what was the largest advertising acquisition in history. This purchase made Saatchi & Saatchi the largest advertising firm in the world at the time.

In addition to advertising, Saatchi & Saatchi also does business in communications services, public relations, and consulting. The Saatchi & Saatchi holding company owns 70% of the Facilities Group, which provides media production services for Saatchi & Saatchi and other customers. The holding company also owns 50% of Zenith Media, a global media buying and coordination agency, and owns Rowland Public Relations, a public relations consulting firm.

As of June 2000, Saatchi & Saatchi is a division of the French ad firm Publicis Groupe, which was interested in Saatchi & Saatchi's strength in the U.S. market. Before the acquisition, Saatchi & Saatchi was ranked as the 12th-largest ad firm in the world. The company creates advertising and public relations campaigns for many of the world's largest multinational corporations, including Visa, Du Pont, Toyota, Kodak, and Procter & Gamble.

Today there are almost 7,000 Saatchi & Saatchi employees in 138 offices in 82 countries. Saatchi & Saatchi currently works for 60 of the world's top 100 advertisers, and its total annual billings are more than $7 billion. Its largest clients, Toyota and Procter & Gamble, account for 20% and 14% of sales, respectively. Saatchi & Saatchi currently generates about 50% of its profits in the U.S., and the rest internationally. As the creator of global corporations' public images, Saatchi & Saatchi and other advertising firms play an important role in how multinationals are viewed by the world.

## Number of Countries in Which 10 Largest Clients Are Represented

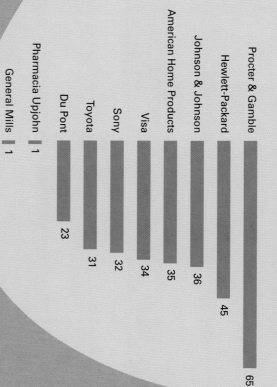

| Client | Number |
| --- | --- |
| Procter & Gamble | 65 |
| Hewlett-Packard | 45 |
| Johnson & Johnson | 36 |
| American Home Products | 35 |
| Visa | 34 |
| Sony | 32 |
| Toyota | 31 |
| Du Pont | 23 |
| Pharmacia Upjohn | 1 |
| General Mills | 1 |

## Regional Revenues 2000
(millions US$)

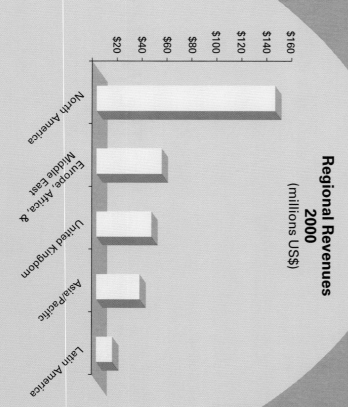

Regions: North America, Europe, Middle East, & Africa, United Kingdom, Asia/Pacific, Latin America

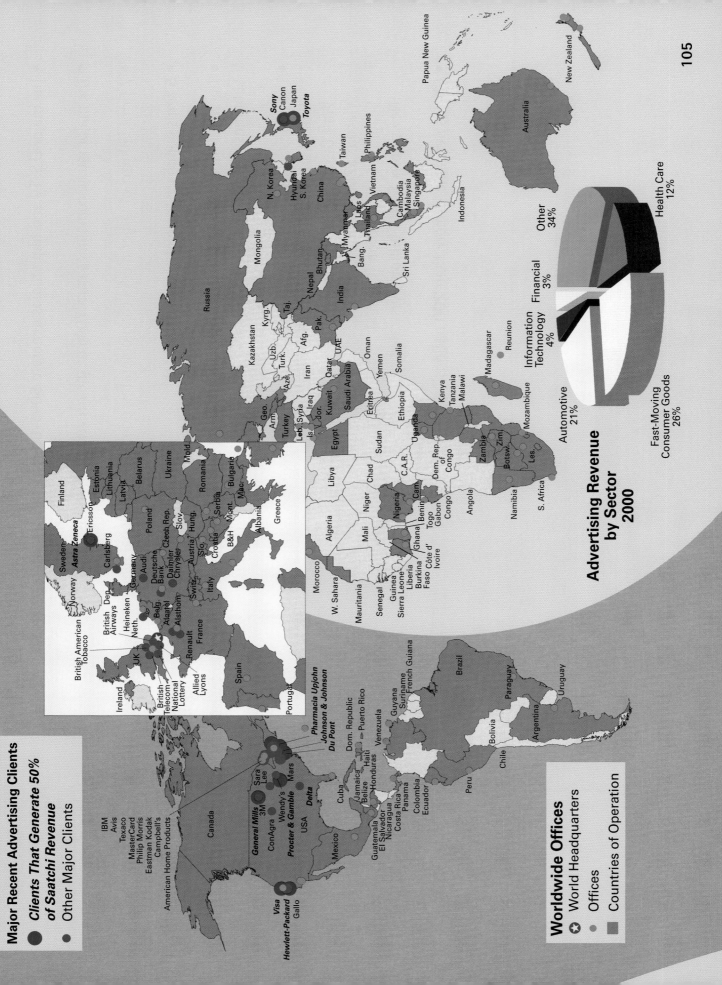

## Major Recent Advertising Clients

- **Clients That Generate 50% of Saatchi Revenue**
- Other Major Clients

IBM
Avis
Texaco
MasterCard
Philip Morris
Eastman Kodak
Campbell's
American Home Products

*General Mills*
3M
Wendy's
*Procter & Gamble*
ConAgra
USA
*Delta*
Mars
Sara
Lee

*Visa*
*Hewlett-Packard*
Gallo

Canada
Mexico
Cuba
Jamaica
Belize
Haiti
Honduras
Guatemala
El Salvador
Nicaragua
Costa Rica
Panama
Dom. Republic
Puerto Rico
Venezuela
Colombia
Ecuador
Guyana
Suriname
French Guiana
Peru
Brazil
Bolivia
Paraguay
Chile
Argentina
Uruguay

*Pharmacia Upjohn*
*Johnson & Johnson*
*Du Pont*

### Worldwide Offices

- ✪ World Headquarters
- • Offices
- ▪ Countries of Operation

### Inset (Europe)

Finland
Sweden
Norway
*Astra Zeneca*
Ericsson
Carlsberg
Estonia
Lithuania
Latvia
Belarus
Ukraine
Mold.
Poland
Audi
Germany
Deutsche Bank
*Daimler Chrysler*
Czech Rep.
Slov.
Austria
Hung.
Romania
Serbia
Bulgaria
Mac.
Mont.
B&H
Croatia
Switz.
Italy
Slo.
Albania
Greece
British Dep.
Airways
Heineken
Neth.
Belg.
*Alcatel*
Alsthom
France
Renault
Allied
Lyons
British American
Tobacco
UK
British
Telecom
National
Lottery
Ireland
Spain
Portugal

Morocco
W. Sahara
Algeria
Libya
Egypt
Mauritania
Mali
Niger
Chad
Sudan
Eritrea
Ethiopia
Somalia
Senegal
Guinea
Sierra Leone
Liberia
Burkina
Faso
Côte d' Ivoire
Ghana
Togo
Benin
Nigeria
Cam.
C.A.R.
Gabon
Congo
Dem. Rep. of Congo
Uganda
Kenya
Tanzania
Rwanda
Malawi
Angola
Zambia
Zim.
Mozambique
Botsw.
Namibia
Les.
S. Africa
Madagascar
Reunion
Yemen
Oman
UAE
Qatar
Saudi Arabia
Kuwait
Iraq
Jor.
Syria
Leb.
Is.

Russia
Mongolia
Kazakhstan
Uzb.
Kyrg.
Turk.
Aze.
Geo.
Arm.
Turkey
Iran
Afg.
Pak.
Taj.
Nepal
Bhutan
India
Bang.
Myanmar
China
N. Korea
S. Korea
*Hyundai*
Japan
*Sony*
Canon
*Toyota*
Taiwan
Sri Lanka
Laos
Thailand
Vietnam
Cambodia
Malaysia
Singapore
Indonesia
Philippines
Papua New Guinea
Australia
New Zealand

### Advertising Revenue by Sector 2000

- Other 34%
- Health Care 12%
- Financial 3%
- Information Technology 4%
- Automotive 21%
- Fast-Moving Consumer Goods 26%

# Media and Entertainment

- The major U.S. TV and film studios generate **50%–60%** of their revenues overseas.

- The major music companies earn **70%** of their revenues overseas.

- **7 firms**, all part of larger media conglomerates, dominate the global film market.

- **5 firms** dominate the global music industry.

- The major Hollywood studios expect to generate **$11 billion** from global TV rights to their film libraries in 2002, up from **$7 billion** in 1998.

- The largest media companies in terms of 2000 assets were:
  Time Warner **$28.5 billion** (U.S.)
  Walt Disney **$25.4 billion** (U.S.)
  Viacom **$20.0 billion** (U.S.)
  Seagram **$14.8 billion** (Canada)
  News Corp. **$14.1 billion** (Australia)

- CNN is available in more than **200** nations.

**North America**
Time Warner  New York, NY
Walt Disney  Burbank, CA
Viacom  New York, NY
Cox  Atlanta, GA
Thomson Corporation  Toronto, Ontario
Tribune Company  Chicago, IL
Hearst Corporation  New York, NY
Bull Run  Atlanta, GA

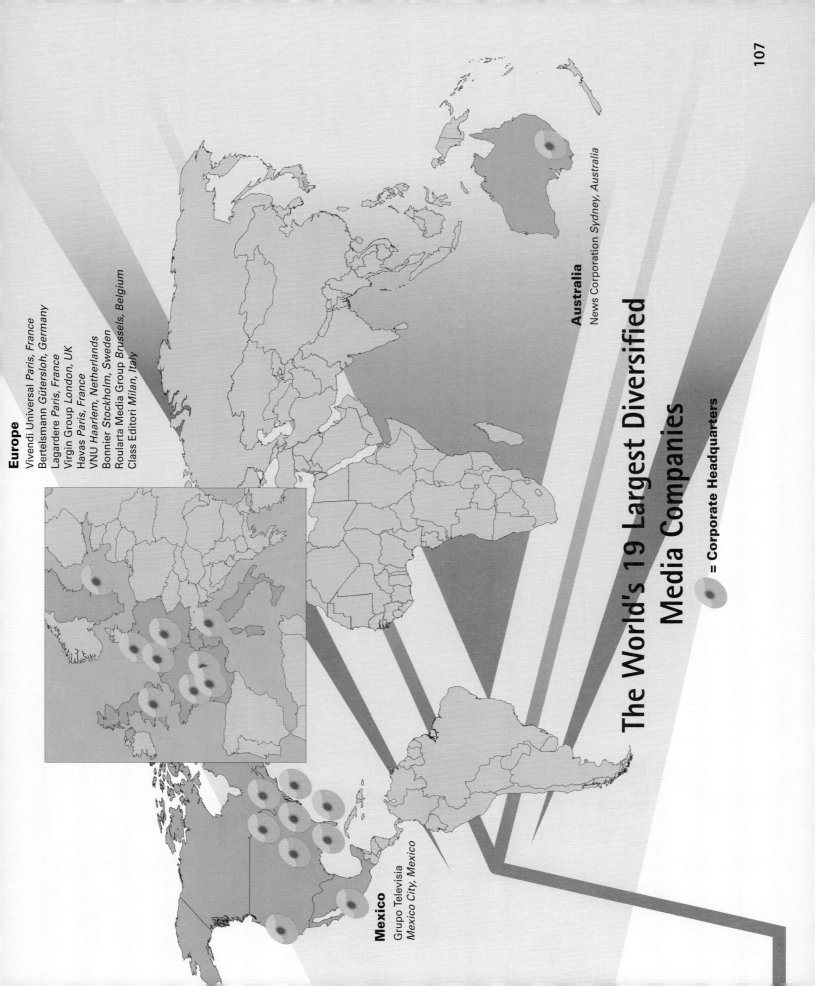

# The World's 19 Largest Diversified Media Companies

● = Corporate Headquarters

**Europe**

Vivendi Universal *Paris, France*
Bertelsmann *Gütersloh, Germany*
Lagardere *Paris, France*
Virgin Group *London, UK*
Havas *Paris, France*
VNU *Haarlem, Netherlands*
Bonnier *Stockholm, Sweden*
Roularta Media Group *Brussels, Belgium*
Class Editori *Milan, Italy*

**Australia**

News Corporation *Sydney, Australia*

**Mexico**

Grupo Televisia
*Mexico City, Mexico*

# Bertelsmann

## Global Expansion 1835–2001

The Bertelsmann firm was founded with Carl Bertelsmann's creation of Bertelsmann Verlag, a small religious publishing company that evolved from a bookbindery to a printing house and finally a full-scale publishing house in Germany in 1835. The hymnal *Theomele* was the company's first bestseller. Bertelsmann steadily diversified into fiction and nonfiction works as well as a newspaper, but theological works remained the firm's focus. Bertelsmann survived World War I and the ensuing hyperinflation in Germany when World War II began. Although the company's leader was a staunch opponent of Hitler, Bertelsmann was still doing a brisk business selling large numbers of cheap books and pamphlets to the German air force.

Bertelsmann faced a number of difficulties during World War II. Initially, the company was forbidden by the Nazi authorities to publish theological texts. The company was also denied sufficient paper by the German rationing authorities, which made it difficult to continue operations. In 1945, Allied bombing destroyed most of Bertelsmann's buildings. The company was rebuilt from this low point when Reinhard Mohn, the son of the current firm president, returned from a Kansas POW camp and took charge.

Bertelsmann started Germany's first book club in 1951 to stimulate sales. Within a year the book club boasted 100,000 members and by 1954 claimed 1 million members. Bertelsmann also began to diversify into other forms of modern media by buying troubled companies in the magazine, television, and record businesses. Over the next 30 years, the company grew at a tremendous rate. The book club continued to grow, and Bertelsmann expanded from 500 employees in 1951 to more than 11,000 in 1973.

The company's acquisitions were soon made on an international scale, allowing it to establish itself in the United States, the world's largest media market. During the 1980s, Bertelsmann acquired two major American publishing companies, Bantam Books and Doubleday, as well as the record companies Arista and RCA. The firm's U.S. publishing business was consolidated under Bantam Doubleday Dell, while its global music business was combined into the Bertelsmann Music Group (BMG).

Bertelsmann continued to expand by acquiring newspapers, magazines, television stations, and radio and book clubs throughout Spain and eastern and central Europe. In 1997 Bertelsmann reached further still to bring the first book club to China. The company acquired Random House Publishing in 1998, which made Bertelsmann the largest publishing interest in the English-speaking world.

Bertelsmann did not ignore the advent of the Internet, and partnered with AOL to set up AOL divisions in Germany, France, and the UK. Most recently the company has allied with Napster, a once free peer-to-peer file-sharing program that came under fire for violating intellectual property rights of record companies and musicians. The two companies will seek to create a paid file-sharing system to market media over the Internet, free from pirated content.

Today, Bertelsmann AG is the world's largest publisher and third-largest diversified media company, with 2000 sales of $16.5 billion. The company owns and operates a network of more than 600 companies in 50 countries worldwide, including a number of major record companies; book, magazine, and newspaper publishers; television and radio stations; printing companies; film and television production companies; and book and record clubs. Its RTL group operates 22 TV and 18 radio stations in 10 European countries and produces 11,000 hours of programming in 35 countries worldwide each year. The Gruner+Jahr division publishes 80 magazines and nine newspapers, and the Industry division operates 18 printing companies throughout the world.

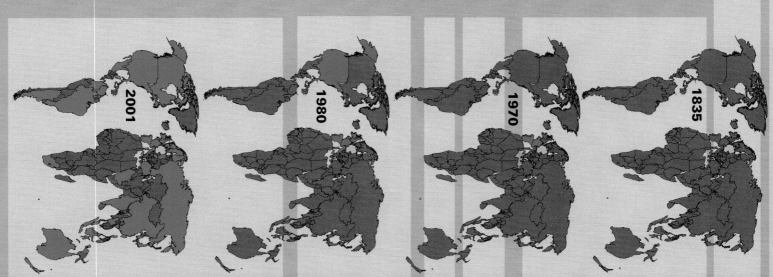

2001

1980

1970

1835

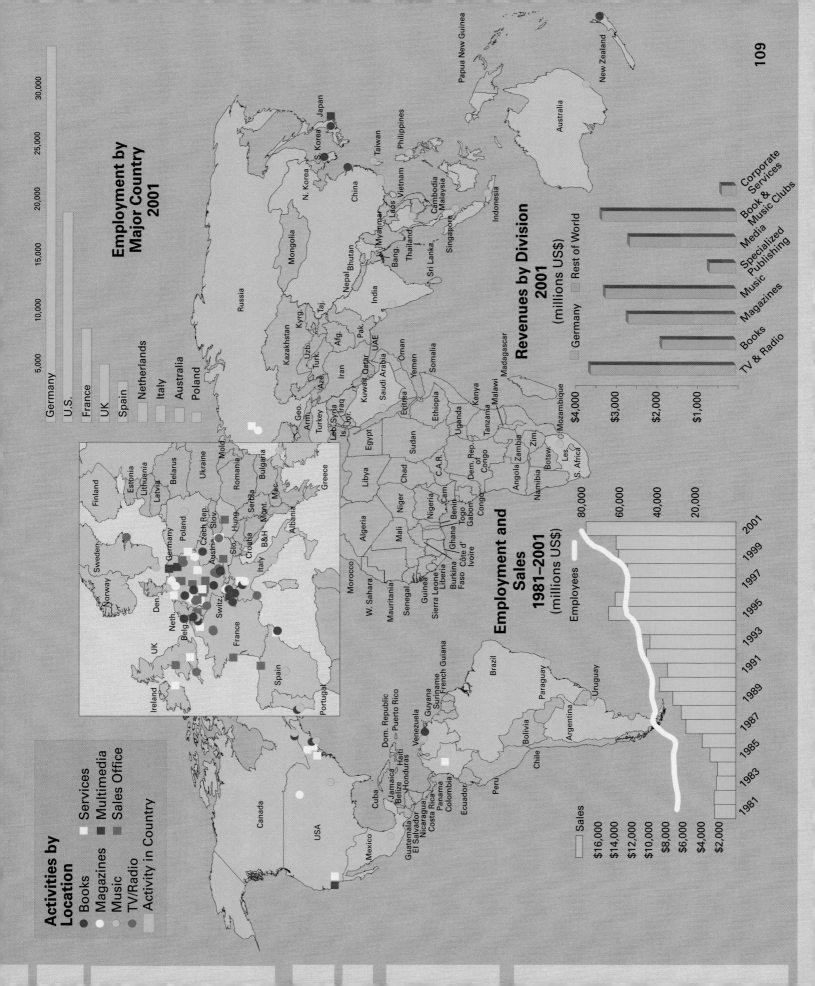

**Activities by Location**
- ● Books
- ○ Magazines
- ○ Music
- ● TV/Radio
- ▦ Activity in Country
- ● Services
- ◼ Multimedia
- ◼ Sales Office

**Employment by Major Country 2001**

- Germany
- U.S.
- France
- UK
- Spain
- Netherlands
- Italy
- Australia
- Poland

5,000  10,000  15,000  20,000  25,000  30,000

**Revenues by Division 2001**
(millions US$)

- Germany
- Rest of World

$1,000  $2,000  $3,000  $4,000

- TV & Radio
- Books
- Magazines
- Music
- Specialized Publishing
- Media
- Book & Music Clubs
- Corporate Services

**Employment and Sales 1981–2001**
(millions US$)

- Employees

20,000  40,000  60,000  80,000

- Sales

$2,000  $4,000  $6,000  $8,000  $10,000  $12,000  $14,000  $16,000

1981  1983  1985  1987  1989  1991  1993  1995  1997  1999  2001

# AOL Time Warner

The history of media giant AOL Time Warner is the story of its three founding firms: Time, Inc., Warner Brothers, and AOL. Warner Brothers was incorporated in 1923 by four brothers to produce and market early films. In 1927, the company produced *The Jazz Singer*, the world's first genuine talking picture. The success of sound movies propelled Warner Brothers to become a major motion-picture studio by 1930. Meanwhile, two Yale University graduates had produced the first issue of the news magazine *Time* in 1923; by 1927 it had a circulation of more than 175,000. The magazine's format became the the de facto standard for other similar magazines, and *Time* continued its success in the following decades. Other magazines were added under the *Time* umbrella over the years, most notably *Fortune* and *Life* in the 1930s, *Sports Illustrated* in 1954, and *People* in 1974.

By the 1970s, Warner Brothers had diversified into television, music recording, and publishing. Time, Inc., had also diversified into cable television with the establishment of HBO and the acquisition of the Turner Networks. In 1989 the two firms merged to form Time Warner, the largest media and entertainment company in the world.

On May 24, 1985, the company now known as America Online was incorporated under its founding name, Quantum Computer Services. In November of that year, Quantum's first on-line service, "Q-Link," was launched for Commodore Business Machines. AOL had its initial public offering in 1992 and then released AOL for Windows in January 1993. The company rapidly gained 500,000 subscribers and was growing exponentially. In 1994 AOL began to acquire Internet technology companies and expand its operations.

AOL became international in 1995 when the first overseas local-language and local-content AOL service was launched in Germany. AOL UK, Canada, and France began in 1996, and Japan was added in 1997. AOL has also launched subsidiaries in Australia, Hong Kong, Brazil, Mexico, and Argentina, largely through joint ventures with Bertelsmann AG in Europe, Mitsui & Co. in Japan, and other international partners. Membership increased from more than 19 million in 1999 to more than 27 million in 2000. Today AOL International offers localized services

in 17 countries and six languages through joint ventures. Additionally, AOL users can access AOL from more than 100 countries and 1,500 cities via AOL GlobalNet.

In January 2001, AOL merged with the Time Warner media corporation in the largest merger in U.S. history. The merger was opposed on antitrust grounds by Walt Disney, Microsoft, AT&T, and other media and Internet concerns. Time Warner controls the second largest cable system in the U.S., and critics worried that AOL Time Warner would be able to deny access to the burgeoning broadband media market. In response to these concerns, regulators imposed strictures on the new company that are supposed to ensure fair competition. The fact remains, however, that the two companies have a huge share of both the content and the distribution of media markets in the U.S.: 78.3 million Internet visitors in October 2000, 19% of cable subscribers, about 15% of music and movies sales, and more than 20% of magazine ad revenue.

AOL Time Warner is a new breed of Internet-powered global media corporation. The firm has worldwide interests in a number of Internet ventures, film and television production, television and cable networks, music, and publishing. The company's Turner Broadcasting System produces the CNN News Group, HBO, and the Cartoon Network, among many other networks. AOL Time Warner also publishes more than 60 magazines.

AOL Time Warner's brands "touch consumers more than 2.5 billion times each month," according to company literature. Between AOL, magazines, and cable, the company has more than 130 million subscriptions. One of the more potent forces of globalization, CNN, is available to at least a billion people worldwide in 212 countries. Warner Music Group owns more than 1 million music copyrights in 68 countries. Only time will tell if the effects of the merger will stop at advertisements for Warner movies and music groups on AOL, or whether the giant media company will exercise an increasingly overpowering control over media content and distribution.

## AOL Global Expansion 1995–2000

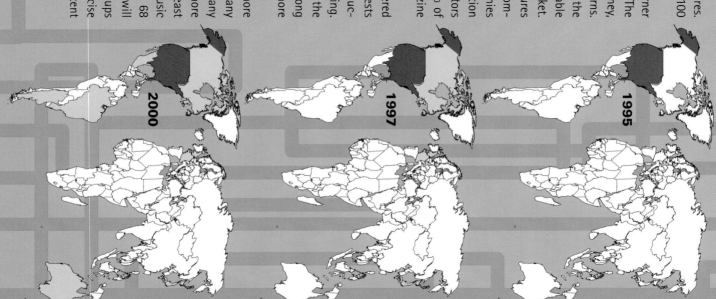

1995

1997

2000

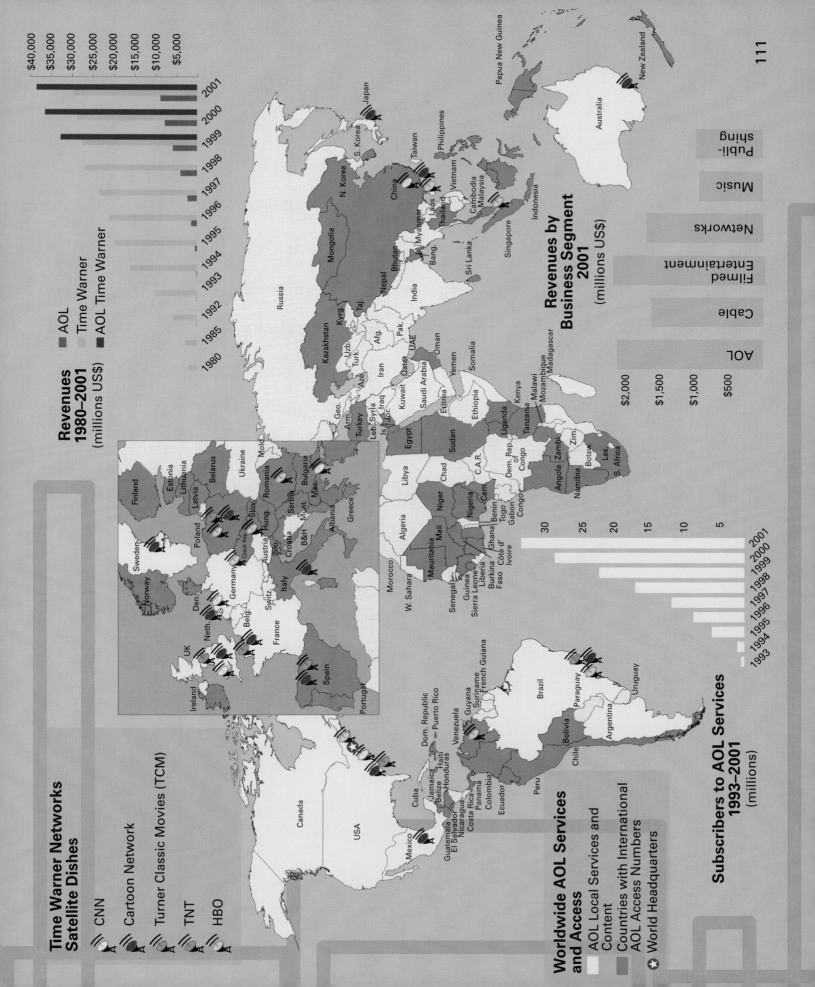

# Time Warner Networks Satellite Dishes

CNN

Cartoon Network

Turner Classic Movies (TCM)

TNT

HBO

# Revenues 1980–2001
(millions US$)

- AOL
- Time Warner
- AOL Time Warner

$40,000
$35,000
$30,000
$25,000
$20,000
$15,000
$10,000
$5,000

1980  1985  1992  1993  1994  1995  1996  1997  1998  1999  2000  2001

## Revenues by Business Segment 2001
(millions US$)

AOL  Cable  Filmed Entertainment  Networks  Music  Publi-shing

$2,000
$1,500
$1,000
$500

# Worldwide AOL Services and Access

- AOL Local Services and Content
- Countries with International AOL Access Numbers
- World Headquarters

## Subscribers to AOL Services 1993–2001
(millions)

30  25  20  15  10  5

1993  1994  1995  1996  1997  1998  1999  2000  2001

# Consulting and Accounting

- Since 1990 revenues in the management consulting industry have been growing by **10%** or more a year, and are up by as much as **20%–30%** at the leading companies.

- The global management consulting market grew from **$120 billion** in 2001 to **$127** billion in 2002, and is forecast to reach **$205 billion** in 2005.

- Because of high demand and a **15%** turnover rate, approximately **33%** of all management consultants are new at what they are doing.

- The "Big Five" firms dominate consulting and accounting industries worldwide. In terms of 2001 revenues, the Big Five are:

  PricewaterhouseCoopers  **$24 billion**
  Deloitte Touche Tohmatsu  **$12.4 billion**
  KPMG  **$11.7 billion**
  Ernst and Young  **$10 billion**
  Aurthur Andersen **$9.3 billion**

- Consultants serve a number of industries globally, including (as % of world consulting revenues, 2000):

  Financial services  **24.7%**
  Manufacturing  **21.2%**
  Communication  **12.1%**
  Business Services  **11.1%**
  Government/Public Sector  **7.6%**
  Wholesale and Retail  **7.2%**
  Transportation  **6.7%**
  Media/Publishing/Entertainment  **3.3%**
  Other  **6.1%**

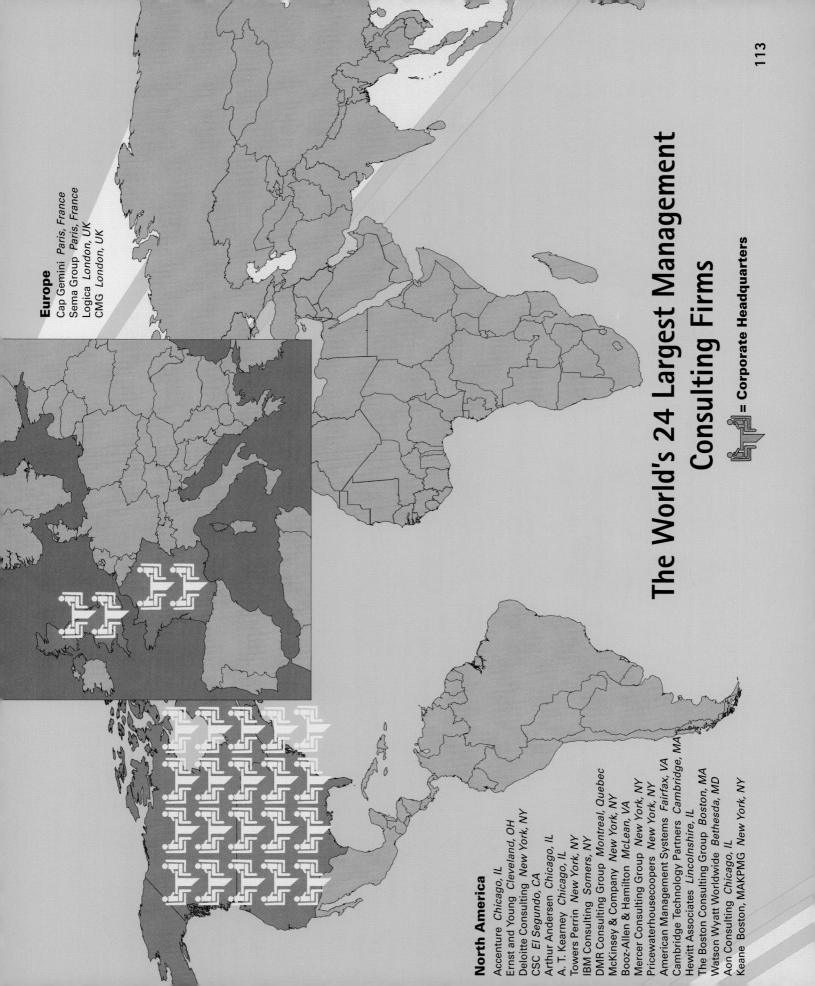

## The World's 24 Largest Management Consulting Firms

**Europe**
Cap Gemini  *Paris, France*
Sema Group  *Paris, France*
Logica  *London, UK*
CMG  *London, UK*

**North America**
Accenture  *Chicago, IL*
Ernst and Young  *Cleveland, OH*
Deloitte Consulting  *New York, NY*
CSC  *El Segundo, CA*
Arthur Andersen  *Chicago, IL*
A. T. Kearney  *Chicago, IL*
Towers Perrin  *New York, NY*
IBM Consulting  *Somers, NY*
DMR Consulting Group  *Montreal, Quebec*
McKinsey & Company  *New York, NY*
Booz-Allen & Hamilton  *McLean, VA*
Mercer Consulting Group  *New York, NY*
Pricewaterhousecoopers  *New York, NY*
American Management Systems  *Fairfax, VA*
Cambridge Technology Partners  *Cambridge, MA*
Hewitt Associates  *Lincolnshire, IL*
The Boston Consulting Group  *Boston, MA*
Watson Wyatt Worldwide  *Bethesda, MD*
Aon Consulting  *Chicago, IL*
Keane  *Boston, MA* KPMG  *New York, NY*

= Corporate Headquarters

# Arthur Andersen/Accenture

The founder of Arthur Andersen was Arthur Edward Andersen. In 1908 he became the youngest CPA in Illinois at age 23. In 1913 he started the accounting firm of Andersen, Delany & Company in Chicago. The firm grew rapidly and established an impressive clientele including ITT, Colgate-Palmolive, Schlitz Brewing, and a score of utility companies. In 1917, the partnership between Andersen and DeLany ended and the firm became Arthur Andersen & Co.

Andersen opened 10 offices nationwide during the 1920s and 1930s. The company also gained a reputation as a sort of overseer of the accounting industry's methods, largely through its success in supervising the reorganization and refinancing of a large network of utilities on the verge of bankruptcy. The company added financial investigations to its list of services, which formed the basis for its future strength in management consulting.

After Andersen's death in 1947, the company continued to thrive under new leadership. The 1950s and early 1960s saw rapid expansion both domestically and abroad. There were 18 new offices in the U.S. and, beginning with a Mexico City office, 26 new offices internationally. As the company grew, it worked to establish standardized practices for the rapidly expanding financial accounting industry. The firm adopted these practices but did not meet with much success in standardizing the industry overall.

By the 1970s, Andersen had become one of the world's leading accounting firms and had developed a successful consulting branch as well. The accounting side provided accounting, auditing, and tax services as well as financial investigations. The consulting arm specialized in management and technology-consulting services. Andersen consultants had established the first computer dedicated to business functions for General Electric in 1953; by 1979 more than 20% of the company's revenues were from consulting services, and by 1988 consulting revenues made up more than 40% of total revenues. This made Arthur Andersen the largest management consulting company in the world. To address the

international scope of its business, the company moved its headquarters to Switzerland in 1977.

Tensions arose between the accounting and consulting parts of the business over the control of the ever-larger consulting operations and because consultants tended to earn less than accountants, even though consultants brought in more revenue. As a result, in 1989 the company split into a partnership of two separate divisions, Arthur Andersen (accounting), and Andersen Consulting. The two divisions were coordinated by Andersen Worldwide.

Andersen Consulting continued to grow through the early 1990s, until it finally grew larger than its progenitor. In 1997 the consulting division decided to end the partnership with the company's accounting branch. After arbitration by the International Chamber of Commerce, the partnership officially dissolved in August 2000.

Andersen Consulting changed its name to Accenture in January 2001, and Arthur Andersen is continuing its accounting and financial services as simply Andersen.

Today the two companies continue to handle the financial, managerial, and technical consulting needs of many of the world's businesses and largest multinational corporations. Andersen has more than 70,000 employees in 385 offices in 85 countries. In 2000, the company generated $8.3 billion in revenue. Andersen was the accounting firm in charge of auditing the Enron Corporation, which went bankrupt in 2002 under a cloud of accusations of financial mismanagement and dishonesty. As a result, Andersen and the entire corporate accounting industry are under intense scrutiny. Andersen's culpability, and therefore financial vulnerability in the Enron debacle, poses a grave risk to the entire corporation.

Accenture is the largest business consulting firm in the world. It has more than 75,000 employees in 47 countries, working in 110 offices. Year 2000 revenues were more than $9.7 billion. Accenture has more than 4,500 clients, including 91 of the world's 100 largest corporations. The company provides consulting services in dozens of areas, including business reorganization, data systems design, outsourcing, e-commerce, and customer service systems.

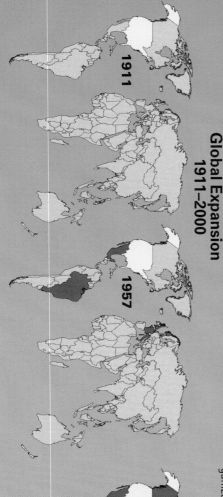

**Global Expansion
1911–2000**

1911

1957

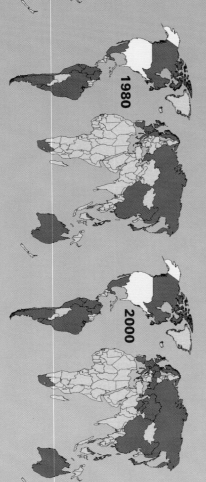

1980

2000

*The expanding array of global opportunities for multinational corporations to transfer money, capital, and technology around the world renders more difficult the reconciliation of the long-term public interest with short-term MNC interests.*

—Eric Kolodner, *Transnational Corporations: Impediments or Catalysts of Social Development?*

# Possible Policies and Actions

*Policy makers urgently need a new mindset if they are to maintain a reasonable equity in the balance of power among states, firms, and consumers. Just as domestic banks require regulatory institutions that restrain their speculative instincts, MNCs require regulatory mechanisms that check their instincts to put profit above all else.*

—John Stopford, *Foreign Policy*

**Actions that countries can take to discourage corporations:**

- Block foreign direct investment.
- Block foreign investment in certain industries.
- Limit overall share of ownership by outside investors.
- Limit investment share of ownership in certain industries.
- Limit ownership of voting shares.
- Nationalize or threaten to nationalize property.
- Levy high or arbitrary taxes.
- Limit/prosecute action under antitrust statutes.
- Extort bribes.
- Impose import tariffs and quantity restrictions on imports.
- Impose steep port charges.
- Impose labor regulations, such as a high minimum wage, safety regulations, right to unionize and strike.
- Impose environmental regulations, in areas such as solid-waste disposal, hazardous-waste disposal, air pollution, water pollution, and noise pollution.
- Impose price controls.
- Impose local-content requirements.
- Require permits for certain types of investment (e.g., building a dam).
- Require building permits/impose zoning restrictions.
- Impose restrictions/prohibitions on acquiring real estate.
- Impose restrictions on establishing a company.
- Do not vigorously enforce and protect contracts.
- Provide an inefficient, poorly-paid civil service.
- Change policy frequently/do not provide a stable playing field.
- Bias policy toward favorites/do not provide a level playing field.

Governments and corporations need each other. Governments need the investment, jobs, taxes, products, innovation, and competency of the corporation to keep their economies vibrant and healthy in today's dynamic and competitive global economy. Corporations need governments to provide the stable playing field and the rule of law so that they can make informed investment decisions about risks and rewards in the same global economy. Corporations also need governments to provide legitimate access to protected markets and resources and to uses of new technology in new markets (such as band-width for cell phone use), and to provide protection from "thieves"—be they in the nature of intellectual property infringement or highway bandits.

## The Need for Governance

Governance is multidimensional, overlapping, and interconnected. There is not one system of governance for all the governments of the world, nor is there (or should there be) a single set of regulations or laws for multinational corporations. There are overlapping systems of personal and professional ethics, guidelines, regional procedures, local customs, national laws, international regulations, industry standards, corporate guidelines, and assorted other "laws" both written and unwritten that guide complex corporate behavior in complicated situations in differing parts of the world under varying circumstances.

All of these various forms of corporate governance are interwoven with the governance of countries. Both are so interconnected that it is not possible to deal with one without also impacting and changing the other. Just as the civil rights movement that swept across the U.S. in the 1960s changed the entire U.S. society, both African American and white, and the women's movement of the 1970s changed men and their relationships with the women in their lives as profoundly as it impacted women, so too will any alteration to the governance of multinational corporations impact and change the governance of countries.

Some changes can already be seen in the lessening of state control over any given country's economy. But there are other changes that countries need to actively undertake if the effective governance of multinational corporations is to move forward. Some changes may be welcomed, and others may be resisted. But as global society continues to deal with the governance of multinational corporations, it will soon realize that the "multinational" part of this process will have profound implications for the governments of the world. In essence, we cannot "govern" the world's multinational corporations unless we also come to grips with governing our now globally interconnected countries. For example, laws requiring transparency of corporate actions will not work in a system where national governments and their leaders can hide information for their own gain. The sword of transparency cuts both ways.

# Governance of the Global Corporation

Possible governance actions needed to make MNCs more responsible and responsive to the needs of global and local societies, the environment, and the economy, as well as to make government/MNC/NGO interaction more fruitful, include:

## 1. International Cooperation

International cooperation among countries to limit or stop the pitting of one country against another (whereby multinational corporations strive to minimize their tax obligations and maximize state subsidies). This can be furthered through:

A. Regional and global economic ministerial meetings where draft environmental, labor, and tax standards are developed and approved and other cooperative actions are taken.

B. The development of an Internet-based database where countries share information about corporate activities.

C. The development of standardized laws that govern property and contract; financial regulation; securities; labor standards; environmental regulation; health and safety standards disclosure and transparency; taxes; and standards of behavior concerning employees, the environment, products provided and services rendered, investments and stockholders, and liability.

## 2. MNC Transparency and Information

A. The development and publication of a "name and shame" blacklist that will identify countries that do not comply with international standards of responsible corporate behavior.

B. The development and publication of a noncooperative multinational corporation "name and shame" blacklist that will identify corporations that do not comply with international standards of responsible corporate behavior regarding the above standards.

C. The development and global ratification of disclosure standards that require every corporation that does business in two or more countries to disclose labor practices and environmental impacts; the Global Reporting Initiative (GRI), where corporations collect data and report on specific social, economic, and environmental impacts that result from corporate processes, products, or services should be standard procedures for all MNCs.

D. The worldwide collection and publishing of data on wages and taxes paid by MNCs throughout the world.

E. The worldwide collection and publishing of data on environmental impacts by MNCs throughout the world.

F. The development of international standards in transparent transnational financial transactions including the ratification of the G-7 finance ministers' "Ten Key Principles on Information Sharing and Disclosure" that pertain to cross-border transactions.

G. Research on environmental and social impacts of MNC activity in developing countries, to identify "best practices" in regards to social/environmental impacts.

H. Corporations should be required to switch auditors every three years.

I. Corporate executives should be required to immediately disclose when they sell or purchase their company's stock.

J. Accounting firms should not be allowed to provide consulting services for corporations they also audit.

---

It is in everyone's interest to have a *global* system of governance for multinational corporations in place as quickly as possible. Citizens and their local and national governments would benefit from regulations that curtailed and then stopped the negative practices and impacts that MNCs have on local and national economies, such as nonsustainable resource use and poor labor standards.

Corporations would benefit from a level playing field and the stability that would provide. Investment decisions that did not have to be second-guessed, factoring in the unknown or whimsical political changes that might change the basic assumptions on which decisions are made, would be extraordinarily helpful.

Multinational governance needs to be seen from the perspective of the long-term best interests of human beings: what policies, regulations, and actions will lead to longer life expectancy, higher quality of life, a healthier environment, and a greater degree of freedom for ever more people. The world needs a set of global regulations for multinational organizations—not to control them, but to enhance their power to do good. The world also needs a countervailing set of global regulations for governments and nongovernmental organizations—one that enhances their powers to work together, along with corporations, to make the world a better place.

Globally sustainable economic and social development is in everyone's best interests. It is easy to say that solutions to the world's problems need to be economically viable, socially responsible and just, and environmentally sustainable. It is going to be harder arriving at a consensus on how to achieve these lofty goals. Given that the Uruguay Round of GATT took more than 11 years to reach its conclusions, now is the time to move toward a system of multinational governance with which we can not only live, but live ever better.

The following list is offered as a departure point for thinking about the set of problems under the rubric of multinational governance. It is not intended as a definitive list but rather as a set of examples of the kinds of actions that should be considered and debated by governments, civil society, and corporations. It is hoped that such discussions will lead to actions and policies that improve the functioning of multinational corporations as agents for positive and sustainable economic, social, and environmental improvement throughout the world.

### 3. Global MNC Tax Code

A. The development of an internationally accepted definition of taxable income.

B. The development of international codes of taxation.

C. The ending of unregulated offshore tax havens.

D. The development of a global tax information center for use by governments as a vehicle to exchange corporate tax information by tax authorities.

E. The institution of a tax on speculative financial transactions (the so-called Tobin tax) as a means of reining in private global money markets. (Close to $1.5 trillion per day is speculated in foreign-exchange transactions.) A tax of one-quarter of 1% on these transactions would raise $750 billion per year;[29] Such revenues could be used to train workers displaced by globalization.

### 4. Global MNC Labor Code

A. The development and global ratification of a Living Wage Code that requires multinational corporations and their subcontractors to pay a living wage, defined as a wage that is equal to the top third of the host country's wage scale, or 150% above minimum levels of poverty in the host country.

B. The elimination of child labor.

C. The development and implementation of global standards for internal safety audits and continuous worker safety training in all MNCs in developing countries.

### 5. Global MNC Employee Health-Care Code

A. The development and global ratification of health-care standards that require multinational corporations and their subcontractors to pay health-care costs for their workers.

### 6. Global MNC Environmental Code

A. The implementation of a two-tiered environmental performance program that provides additional motivation and reward for MNC corporations that are high environmental performers. One such system would have a Tier 1 that would recognize performance of companies that have a consistent compliance record, an environmental management system, and a commitment to continued environmental improvement and public outreach; Tier 2 would target exemplary facilities as models of best practices in their respective industries.[30]

B. All MNCs doing business in three or more countries should be required to be ISO 14001 certified.

C. Develop incentives for implementing the Kyoto Protocol on Climate Change.

D. The Basel Convention, which deals with cross-border shipments of hazardous waste and which went into force in 1992, should be strengthened to further protect developing countries.

### 7. Global MNC Government Relations Code

All MNCs doing business in three or more countries should be required to sign a code of conduct that requires them to:[31]

A. Respect national sovereignty.

B. Refrain from interfering in a government's internal affairs, and refrain from making direct or indirect political contributions.[32]

C. Adhere to a host government's economic, social, and cultural objectives.

D. Renegotiate contracts signed under duress.

E. Respect human and worker rights.

F. Abstain from corrupt practices.

G. Facilitate local employment.

H. Cooperate on balance-of-payments issues.

I. Refrain from transfer pricing and anticompetitive practices.

J. Foster transfer of technology.

K. Promote consumer and environmental protection.

L. Disclose relevant information.

Host governments in return should:

A. Grant MNCs fair and equitable treatment.

B. Provide adequate compensation for nationalized or expropriated property.

C. Establish rights to transfer all payments legally due.

D. Disclose all relevant information on laws and administration policies in a timely manner.

E. Ensure the confidentiality of MNC-disclosed materials.

F. Facilitate the transfer of MNC employees between divisions of the corporation.

G. Establish laws for banking, bankruptcy, and contracts.

H. Establish business codes of conduct.

I. Conform to international accounting standards.

J. Establish regulatory oversight agencies.

K. Establish laws against conflict of interest and insider trading by government officials.

### 8. World Trade Organization Improvements

A. All World Trade Organization operations and decisions should be transparent so that public trust is restored and strengthened.

B. Regulations for MNCs should be developed that incorporate the above Transparency, Tax, Labor, Health Care, and Environmental codes.

C. Regulations should be developed and implemented that require MNCs to both assist developing countries in which they do business in implementing ISO 14001 certification programs, and to then help local partners and subsidiaries to become ISO certified.

D. Corporations should be prohibited from seeking or accepting "incentive" packages from any government. Such "incentive" packages should be defined by the WTO as part of this regulation.

E. Rules of evidence, due process, public hearings, and restrictions on conflicts of interest should be developed and implemented.

## 9. MNCs and Criminal Justice

A. International criminal law should cover MNCs, and the International Criminal Court should have its jurisdiction expanded to cover corporate conduct.

B. The 1999 European Code of Conduct for European MNCs Operating Abroad should be enforced by the European Union and have the force of law.

C. Increased funding for enforcement of existing environmental and human rights laws to reduce and stop, for example, the estimated $15 billion per year trafficking in toxic waste, the $500 billion in annual retail sales of illegal drugs, and the $10 billion per year illegal trade in endangered species.[33]

D. "Three strikes and you're out": three felony convictions and the corporation's charter is revoked.

E. All corporate records and documents should be open to the state attorney.

F. Corporations should be required to have their headquarters and meetings in the place where their principal place of business is located.

G. The double standard in criminal justice should be reversed. In the U.S. S&L debacle of the 1980s and 1990s, convicted felons (who often defrauded depositors and the government of millions, sometimes hundreds of millions, of dollars) received on average 36.4 months of jail time—contrasted with thieves who stole $300 or less and first-time drug offenders, who received 65 months.[34]

## 10. MNCs and Education

A. Investments in education by multinational corporations and governments should be encouraged in every developing country they do business in to add value to a country's labor force.

## 11. World Financial Authority

A. The institution of a "World Financial Authority" to "perform in the domain of world financial markets what national regulators do in domestic markets."[35] Such an entity would perform the same tasks as national regulators: information gathering and dissemination, authorization, surveillance, guidance, enforcement, and policy. The goals of such an organization would include slowing down short-term capital speculation and currency trading.

## 12. MNC Standards

A. The Organization for Economic Cooperation and Development (OECD) Guidelines on Multinational Enterprises should be updated (it was formulated in 1976) and strengthened.

B. The International Labor Organization's Tripartite Declaration of Principles Concerning Multinational Enterprise and Social Policy should be updated and strengthened.

C. The International Chamber of Commerce's Business Charter for Sustainable Development should be signed by all MNCs that do business in three or more countries.

D. Corporations should be required to list all product ingredients.

## 13. Corporate Governance

Corporate governance needs to be strengthened through truly independent boards who are responsible for hiring and firing the outside auditor, corporate citizenship, and for malfeasance and financial performance.

The above points are examples of some of the actions that need to be examined, discussed, and debated by governments, civil society, and corporations. They, the major players on the now global stage, need to work together to forge a compact that harnesses the MNCs as engines of prosperity and eliminates their role as ruthless exploiters. Such policies and actions, if implemented, will have a profound impact on the global economy and the positive role of multinational corporations in that economy.

Can the powerful economic development engines of multinational corporations be harnessed for social good as well as increasing shareholder value? Can the enormous capacities for creating products, services, and wealth that multinational corporations possess be used to eliminate poverty and bring the whole world up to a standard of living that generates ever-increasing amounts of wealth? These are the major questions facing us in the global epoch. Stay tuned.

# Notes

## Introduction

1. Kenny Bruno, Joshua Karlinger, and China Brotsky, *Greenhouse Gangsters vs. Climate Justice* (San Francisco: CorpWatch, 1999), p. 6.

## I. Global Inc.

1. "The World's Largest Corporations: *Fortune* 2000 Global 500," *Fortune*, 23 July 2001, pp. F1–F10 (used for corporate revenue); *World Development Report 2001* (Washington, D.C.: World Bank, 2001) (used for country GNP).
2. United Nations Conference on Trade and Development (UNCTAD), *World Investment Report 2001* (New York: United Nations, 2001), p. 9.
3. John Stopford, "Multinational Corporations," *Foreign Policy* 113 (Winter 1998/99), pp.12–24.
4. UNCTAD, *World Investment Report 2001*, p. 239.
5. "The World's Largest Corporations," *Fortune* 2000 Global 500.
6. Ibid. The three corporations are all from China.
7. "A Survey of Multinationals," *The Economist*, 27 March 1993, p. 9.
8. UNCTAD, *World Investment Report 2000* (New York: United Nations, 2000), p. 81.
9. UNCTAD, *World Investment Report 2001*, p. 7.
10. Ibid. (Used for number of MNCs and subsidiaries, 25% of world GDP, employment, wages, and taxes).
11. "The World's View of Multinationals," *The Economist*, 29 January 2000, p. 21.
12. "The World's Largest Corporations," *Fortune* 2000 Global 500.
13. Robert McChesney, "The Political Economy of Global Media," April 1998. www.wacc.org.uk.
14. Correspondence with Alfred Chandler, June 2000.
15. "The World's View of Multinationals," p. 21.
16. Ibid.
17. Ibid.
18. In light of this, it should be remembered that the early multinational corporations engaged in armed conflict and not just economic warfare. India was "conquered" by the mercenary armies of the East India Company, not the army of England or another nation. Today, the internal security force of General Motors is larger than the armies of most countries.

Figure and Map Sources

"The World's 100 Largest Economies": Country GDP: *World Development Indicators on CD-ROM 1999* (Washington D.C.: World Bank, 1999); Corporate Revenue: "The World's Largest Corporations," *Fortune* 2000 Global 500. ● "Number of Countries and Corporations 1900–2000" and "Number of Multinational Corporations 1600–2000": Corporations: Geoffrey Jones, *The Evolution of International Business* (New York: Routledge, 1996); UNCTAD, *World Investment Report*, various years. Countries: "Little Countries: Small but Perfectly Formed," *The Economist*, 1 March 1998, p. 65. ● "Number of Multinational Corporate Headquarters by Country 2000": UNCTAD *World Investment Report 2000*, p. 239. ● "Home Countries of the World's 500 Largest Corporations 2000": See note 1, chapter 1. ● "50 Largest Multinational Corporations from Developing Countries 1999": See note 8, chapter 1. ● "Home Countries of the World's 500 Largest Corporations 1962–1999": 1962: See note 14, chapter 1; 1999: See note 1, chapter 1.

## II. The Foundations of Multinational Corporations: Globalization

1. "One World?" *The Economist*, 18 October 1997, p. 57.
2. Ulrich Beck, *What Is Globalization?* (New York: Polity Press, 2000).
3. Fredric K. Sheppard, "What Is Globalization?" www.cuadralgroup.com/globis.htm.
4. Jeffrey A. Rosensweig, *Winning the Global Game* (New York: The Free Press, 1998).
5. Jeffrey Garten, ed., *World View: Global Strategies for the New Economy* (Boston: Harvard Business School Press, 2000).
6. UNCTAD, *World Investment Report 1999* (New York: United Nations, 1999), p. 17.
7. "Risky Returns," *The Economist*, 20 May 2000, p. 85.

Figure and Map Sources

"Number of Internet Hosts and Cummulative Number of Countries Connected to the Internet 1969–2000": Internet Hosts 1969–1979: "Hobbe's Internet Timeline," www.info.isoc.org/guest/zakon/Internet/History/HIT.htmland; Internet Hosts 1980–2002: "Internet Domain Survey," www.isc.org/ds/host-count-history.html; Cumulative Number of Countries 1969–1985: "NSFNET Networks by Country," www.nic.merit.edu/nsfnet/statistics/nets.by.country; Cummulative Number of Countries 1991–1997: "International Connectivity," ftp://ftp.cs.wisc.edu/connectivity_table/; Cummulative Number of Countries 2002: author's estimate. ● "International Telephone Traffic and Cellular Phone Users 1989–2002: Telegeography, Inc., *Telegeography 2000* (Washington, D.C.: Telegeography, Inc., 2000). ● "Internet Connectivity 1991–2002": "International Connectivity," ftp://ftp.cs.wisc.edu/connectivity_table/. ● "Value of World Trade 1830–1999": Susan Strange, *Paths to International Economy* (Boston: G. Allen & Unwin, 1984). ● "Global Exports As a Percentage of World Output 1870–1996": Rondo L. Cameron, *A Concise Economic History of the World* (New York: Oxford University Press, 1989). ● "Trade As a Percentage of GDP by Country 1960–1998": Albert Kenwood and Allan Lougheed, *The Growth of the International Economy, 1820–2000* (New York: Routledge, 1999). ● "Average Worldwide Tariffs 1947–1990": "Schools Brief: Trade Winds," *The Economist*, 8 November 1997 p. 85. ● "Transnationality Index of Host Countries": UNCTAD, *World Investment Report 1999*, p. 17. ● "Developing Country Investment Risk Index": "Risky Returns," *The Economist*, 20 May 2000, p. 45. ● "GATT/WTO Signatories and Observers 1948–2000" and "Number of Countries in GATT/WTO 1950–2000": World Trade Organization Web site, www.wto.org. ● "Number of Regional Integration Agreements 1948–1999": "World Trade Survey," *The Economist*, 3 October 1998, p. 4.

## III. The History of Multinational Corporations

1. "Silk Road," *Encyclopaedia Britannica* Online Edition, www.britannica.com/bcom.
2. "The Economy of the Roman World," *The Times Atlas of World History* (London: Tim Books, 1978), p. 90.
3. "Ancient Roman Trade," http://pubweb.ucdavis.edu/Documents/ASPANG/Ancient Trade.html.
4. "The Economy of the Roman World," *The Times Atlas of World History*, p. 90.
5. "The Emergence of States in Africa 900 to 1500," *The Times Atlas of World History*, p. 136; "History of North Africa," *Encyclopaedia Britannica* Online Edition, www.britannica.com.
6. Sharon Begley with Erika Check, "The Ancient Mariners," *Newsweek*, 3 April 2000, p. 52.
7. Helena Hertzberg, "The Vikings in Ireland," user.tninet.se/~aww999l/vikings/trade.htm.
8. "The Real Viking Legacy," *Discovering Archeology*, 1 September 2000, p. 14.
9. "European Expansion Overseas," *The Times Atlas of World History*, pp. 158–159.

10. Ibid.

11. "Indian Ocean," *Encyclopaedia Britannica Online Edition*, www.britannica.com.

12. John Dunning, *Multinational Enterprises and the Global Economy* (Wokingham, UK: Addison Wesley, 1993), p. 97.

13. "Merchants and Finance in Europe," *The Times Atlas of World History*, pp. 144–145.

14. Herbert Heaton, *Economic History of Europe* (New York: Harper Brothers, 1936), p. 149.

15. John Dunning, *Multinational Enterprises and the Global Economy*, p. 98.

16. Herbert Heaton, *Economic History of Europe*, pp. 322–323.

17. Ibid., p. 323.

18. "Merchant Adventurers," *Encyclopaedia Britannica Online Edition*, www.britannica.com.

19. Bohdana Hawrylyshyn, "The Internationalization of Firms," *Journal of World Trade Law*, Jan.–Feb. 1971, pp. 72–82.

20. "Those Medici," *The Economist*, 31 December 1999, p. 90.

21. Ibid.

22. "Fugger Family," *Encyclopaedia Britannica Online Edition*, www.britannica.com; Herbert Heaton *Economic History of Europe*, pp. 357–358.

23. George Cawston and Augustus Keane, *The Early Chartered Companies* (New York: Burt Franklin, 1968), pp. 33–35.

24. Ibid., p. 36.

25. Ibid., pp. 33–59.

26. John Dunning, *Multinational Enterprises and the Global Economy*, p. 97.

27. "Dutch East India Company," *Encyclopaedia Britannica Online Edition*, www.britannica.com.

28. "Japan and the VOC in the 17th Century," http://allserv.rug.ac.be/~sdconinc/VOC welcome.htm.

29. "The East India Companies," *The Economist*, 31 December. 1999, p.76.

30. "East India Company," *Encyclopaedia Britannica Online Edition*, www.britannica.com.

31. Ibid.

32. "French East India Company," *Encyclopaedia Britannica Online Edition*, www.britannica.com.

33. Ole Feldbaek, "The Danish Trading Companies of the Seventeenth and the Eighteenth Centuries," *Scandinavian Economic History Review* 34, 3 (1986), pp. 204–218.

34. "Hudson's Bay Company," *Encyclopaedia Britannica Online Edition*, www.britannica.com.

35. "A Brief History of the Hudson's Bay Company," www.gov.mb.ca/chc/archives/hbca/about/ the-bay.html.

36. "History of Western Africa," *Encyclopaedia Britannica Online Edition*, www.britannica.com.

37. Herbert Heaton, *Economic History of Europe*, p. 456.

38. Herbert Heaton, *Economic History of Europe*, p. 456.

39. "Royal African Company Established," www/pbs.org/wgbh/aia/part1/1p269.html.

40. "Jamestown Settlement," "Africans in America: Resource Bank, www.pbs.org/wgbh/aia/ part1/1p261.html.

41. "Massachusetts Bay Company," Infoplease.com Online Encyclopedia, www.infoplease.com/ce5/CE033249.html.

42. "New Sweden," *Encyclopaedia Britannica Online Edition*, www.britannica.com.

43. "New France," *Encyclopaedia Britannica Online Edition*, www.britannica.com.

44. Geoffrey Jones, *The Evolution of International Business* (New York: Routledge, 1996), p. 28.

45. John Dunning, *Multinational Enterprises and the Global Economy*, p. 116.

46. Ibid., p. 105.

47. Ibid., p. 99.

48. William Z. Ripley, "Races in the United States," *Atlantic Monthly*, December 1908, www.theatlantic.com/unbound/flashbks/immigr/rip.htm.

49. Herbert Heaton, *Economic History of Europe*, p. 573.

50. Ibid.

51. Ibid, p. 578.

52. Mira Wilkins, "The Free Standing Company Revisited," in *The Free Standing Company in the World Economy, 1830–1996*, eds. Mira Wilkins and Harm Schroeder (Oxford, UK: Oxford University Press, 1998), p. 8.

53. Geoffrey Jones, *Banks As Multinationals* (New York: Routledge, 1990).

54. John Dunning, *Multinational Enterprises and the Global Economy*, p. 100.

55. John Stopford, cited in ibid., p. 108.

56. Mira Wilkins, *The Emergence of Multinational Enterprise* (Cambridge, Mass.: Harvard University Press, 1970), p. 36.

57. Ibid., pp. 17–18.

58. Mira Wilkins, "History of Multinational Corporations," in *International Encyclopedia of Business and Management*, ed. Malcolm Warner (London: Routledge, 1996), vol. 4, p. 3566.

59. Mira Wilkins, *The Emergence of Multinational Enterprise*, pp. 37–43.

60. Ibid., pp. 45–64.

61. Ibid., pp. 199–204.

62. Mira Wilkins, "History of Multinational Corporations," p. 3567.

63. W. O. Henderson, *The Rise of German Industrial Power, 1834–1914* (London: Temple Smith, 1975), p. 163.

64. Ibid., pp. 186–187.

65. Ibid, pp. 189–192.

66. John Dunning, *Multinational Enterprises and the Global Economy*, p. 105.

67. Alan Milward and S. B. Paul, *The Economic Development of Continental Europe 1780–1870* (Totowa, N.J.: Rowman and Littlefield, 1973), p. 250.

68. Ibid., p. 286.

69. Herbert Heaton, *Economic History of Europe*, p. 631.

70. Ibid.

71. Geoffrey Jones, *The Evolution of International Business*, p. 33.

72. John Dunning, *Multinational Enterprises and the Global Economy*, p. 56.

73. Mira Wilkins, "History of Multinational Corporations," p. 3567.

74. Geoffrey Jones, *The Evolution of International Business*, p. 40.

75. Mira Wilkins, "History of Multinational Corporations," p. 3568.

76. Ibid.

77. Frederick Clairmonte and John Cavanagh, *The World in Their Web: The Dynamics of Textile Multinationals* (London: Zed Press, 1981), pp. 5–6.

78. UNCTAD, *World Investment Report 2001*, p. 9.

79. Ibid.

80. UNCTAD, *World Investment Report 2000*, p. 485.

81. UNCTAD, *World Investment Report 2001*, p. 9.

82. Ibid., p. 89.

83. Ibid., p. 90.

84. UNCTAD, *World Investment Report 2000*, p. 99.

85. Ibid., p. 16.

86. Ibid., p. 52.

87. Ibid.

88. Michael Renner, "Corporations Driving Globalization," in *Vital Signs 1999*, ed., Linda Starke (Washington, D.C.: World Watch Institute, 1999), p. 137.

Figure and Map Sources

"The Opening of World Trade": See notes 1–11, chapter 3. ● "Major European Multinational Business Organizations 1300–1600": See notes 12–25, chapter 3. ● "Rise of Global Trade 1600–1800": See notes 26–43, chapter 3. ● "The First Global Economy 1814–1900": *The Times Atlas of World History*; John Dunning, *Multinational Enterprises and the Global Economy.* ● "Major Powers' Share of World Trade 1840–1913": *The Times Atlas of World History.* ● "World Stock of FDI 1914–1999": Geoffrey Jones, The *Evolution of International Business*; UNCTAD, *World Investment Report*, various years. ● "Number of Multinational Corporate Parent Companies by Country": Geoffrey Jones, *The Evolution of International Business*; Commission of the European Communities, *Survey of International Enterprises* (Brussels, 1976); UNCTAD, *World Investment Report 2000.* ● "Percentage Share of Inward/ Outward FDI Stock 1914–1980": Geoffrey Jones, *The Evolution of International Business 1980–2000*; UNCTAD, *World Investment Report*, various years. ● "Outward Foreign Direct Investment Stock," Annual Average FDI Growth," all "Cross-Border Mergers and Acquisitions" maps and figures: UNCTAD, *World Investment Report*, various years.

## IV. The Global Corporations

Motor Vehicles

"Motor Vehicles," in Scott Heil, ed., *Encyclopedia of Global Industries* (Detroit: Gale, 1999).

General Motors

"General Motors Corporation," *Hoover's Handbook of American Business 1995* (Austin, Tex.: Reference Press, 1995). ● Philip Matera, "General Motors Corporation," in *World Class Business*, ed., Philip Matera (New York: Holt, 1992), p. 314. ● *Moody's Industrial Manual* (New York: Moody's Investors' Service, various years). ● General Motors Corporation, *General Motors International Facts Book* (Detroit: General Motors, 1998). ● General Motors *Annual Report*, various years. ● "GM's Motor Man," *The Economist*, 18 March 2000, p. 69. ● "The World's Largest Corporations," *Fortune 2000* Global 500. ● General Motors Form 10-K, various years, www.sec.gov. ● "Investor Information," www.gm.com/company/investor_ information/. ● *Directory of Corporate Affiliations* (New Providence, N.J.: National Register Publishing, 1999).

Toyota

Philip Matera, "Toyota Corporation," in *World Class Business*, ed., Philip Matera (New York: Holt, 1992). ● *Toyota: A History of the First Fifty Years* (Toyota City, Japan: Toyota Motor Corporation, 1988). ● "The World's Largest Corporations," *Fortune 2000* Global 500. ● Toyota Form "Toyota 2001 Databook," "Investor Information," www.global.toyota.com. ● Toyota Form 10-K, various years, www.sec.gov. ● Toyota *Annual Report*, various years. ● *Directory of Corporate Affiliations* (New Providence, N.J.: National Register Publishing, 1999).

Petroleum and Petrochemicals

"Petroleum," in Scott Heil, ed., *Encyclopedia of Global Industries* (Detroit: Gale, 1999) ● "The Statistical Review of World Energy," 2000 and 2001, BP, www.bp.com/centres/energy/index.asp.

ExxonMobil

"Corporate Overview," www.exxon.mobil.com/overview/. ● "Exxon," *Encyclopaedia Britannica* Online Edition, www.britannica.com. ● *Moody's Industrial Manual* (New York: Moody's Investors' Service, various years). ● Exxon *Annual Report*, various years. ● Exxon and Mobil Form 10-K, various years, www.sec.gov. ● "The World's Largest Corporations," *Fortune 2000* Global 500. ● Jonathan Martin, "Exxon Cor-poration," in *International Directory of Corporate Affiliations*, vol. 7, ed., Paula Kepos (Detroit: St. James Press, 1993), pp. 169–173.

BP

"BP Now Means 'Beyond Petroleum,'" *PHOTON International*, August 2000, p. 2. ● "British Petroleum Company PLC," *Hoover's Handbook of World Business 1992* (Austin, Tex.: Reference Press, 1992). ● Geoffrey Jones, "British Petroleum Company," in *International Directory of Company Histories*, vol. 7, ed, Paula Kepos (Detroit: St. James Press, 1993), pp. 56–59. ● Form 10-K, various years, www.sec.gov. ● "Investor Centre," www.bp.com/investor_centre/index.asp. ● *International Directory of Corporate Affiliations* (New Providence, N.J.: National Register, 1999).

Chemicals and Pharmaceuticals

"Chemical Industry in the Emerging Markets," www.chemb.com/news/chemicalind4.asp. ● "Industrial Chemicals," Scott Heil, ed., *Encyclopedia of Global Industries* (Detroit: Gale, 1999). ● "The World's Largest Corporations," *Fortune 2000* Global 500. ● "Market Report," www.ims-global.com/insight/report/global/report.htm. ● "The Pharmaceutical Industry," *The Economist*, 21 February 1998, p. 56.

Novartis

"Swiss Drug Makers to Merge in One of the Biggest Corporate Deals Ever," *The News–Times: Business News*, 7 March 1996, p. 1. ● "The World's Largest Corporations," *Fortune 2000* Global 500. ● "Ciba-Geigy," *Hoover's Handbook of World Business 1992* (Austin, Tex.: Reference Press, 1992), p. 176. ● "Who We Are: Overview," www.info.novartis.com/ weare/index.html. ● "Novartis AG," *Encyclopaedia Britannica* Online Edition, www.britannica.com. ● A. Dougal, "Ciba," in *International Directory of Company Histories*, vol. 8, ed., Paula Kepos (Detroit: St. James Press, 1994), pp. 108–111. ● "Sandoz," *International Directory of Company Histories*, vol. 1 (Detroit: St. James Press, 1988), pp. 671–673. ● "Sandoz," *Hoover's Handbook of World Business 1992* (Austin, Tex.: Reference Press, 1992), p. 280. ● Sandoz and Ciba-Geigy *Annual Report*, various years. ● "Investor Relations," www.novartis.com/investors/index.shtml.

Du Pont

Doug Gelbert, *So Who the Heck Was Oscar Mayer: The Real People Behind the Name Brands* (New York: Barricade Books, 1996). ● Scott Lewis, "E. I. du Pont de Nemours and Company," in *International Directory of Company Histories*, vol. 8, ed., Paula Kepos (Detroit: St. James Press, 1994), pp. 147–154. ● "History of Du Pont: Modern Materials Revolution," www.dupont.com/corp/gbl-company/. ● "DuPont Sucks," www.dupontsucks.com/. ● Du Pont Form 10-K, various years, www.sec.gov. ● "Davis Tree Farms v. Du Pont (Company Settles Florida Benlate Cases)," www.courttv.com/legaldocs/ business/dupont.html. ● *Moody's Industrial Manual* (New York: Moody's Investors' Service, various years). ● Du Pont *Annual Report*, various years. ● *Directory of Corporate Affiliations* (New Providence, N.J.: National Register Publishing, 1999).

## Construction and Construction Materials

"Hydraulic Cement," "Residential Building Construction," "Non-Residential Building Construction," in Scott Heil, ed., *Encyclopedia of Global Industries* (Detroit: Gale, 1999). • "The World's Largest Corporations," *Fortune* 2000 Global 500.

### CEMEX

"Who We Are: Company Overview," www.cemex.com/english/who/01011.html. • "CEMEX SA de CV (CX)," Market Guide Online, www.marketguide.com/mgi/busidesc.asp?nss=www &rt=busidesc&r. • "Who We Are: Historical Development," www.cemex.com/english/ who/01021.html. • Investor Relations," www.cemex.com/english/ir/15041.html. • CEMEX *Annual Report*, various years.

## Forest and Paper Products

"Pulp Mills," in Scott Heil, ed., *Encyclopedia of Global Industries* (Detroit: Gale, 1999). • "The Emerging Global Paper Industry," http://worldleadersinprint.com/global. • "State of the World's Forests," FAO, www.fao.org/forestry/FO/SOFO/sofo-e.stm. • *World Resources 1999* (Washington, D.C.: World Resources Institute, 1999).

### Sappi

Edward Ryan, "Survey: Forestry–Seed Planted 112 Years Ago," *Business Times South Africa*, 30 April 2000, p. 8. • Philip Gawith, "Gencor Ltd.," in *International Directory of Company Histories*, vol. 4, ed., Adele Hast (Detroit: St. James Press, 1991),pp. 90–93. • Victor Mallet, "The Search for Simplicity," *Financial Times*, 24 May 1999, p. 12. • Hilary Joffe, "Pulp and Paper Duo Storms World Stage," *Business Day South Africa*, 15 October 1997, p. 15. • "Investor Information," Sappi, www.sappi.com/home.asp?pid=483. • "Overseas Bankers Back South African Expansion," *South Africa Business Intelligence*, 24 October 1994. • Sappi *Annual Report* 1999 & 2000. • "Sappi Limited (SPP)," Market Guide Online, www.marketguide.com/mgi/busidesc.asp?nss=www&rt=busidesc&rn=AID6F.

## Trading/Conglomerates

"The World's Largest Corporations," *Fortune* 2000 Global 500. • "Portrait of Tomorrow's Trading Firms," Japan Foreign Trade Council, http://jftc.or.jp. • "Japanese Companies— Their Role in Australian Economic Development," Committee for Economic Development of Australia, www.ceda.com.au.

### Mitsui

"Mitsui Group," *Encyclopaedia Britannica Online Edition*, www.britannica.com. • "The World's Largest Corporations," *Fortune* 2000 Global 500. • "Mitsui's Network," www.mitsui.co.jp/ tkabz/english/investors/. • "Corporate Information: Company Profile," www.mitsui.co.jp/ tkabz/english/corp/index.htm. • *Moody's Industrial Manual* (New York: Moody's Investors' Service, various years). • Mitsui *Annual Report*, various years. • *Hoover's Handbook of World Business* (Austin, Tex.: Reference Press, 1992).

## Computers and Electronics

"PCs-in-Use Surpassed 600M," Computer Industry Almanac, Inc., www.c-i-a.com/. • "Computer Hardware," in Scott Heil, ed., *Encyclopedia of Global Industries* (Detroit: Gale, 1999). • "The World's Largest Corporations," *Fortune* 2000 Global 500. • "2001 Sales Exceed Revised Estimates," Consumer Electronics Association, www.ce.org/newsroom/ newsloader.asp?newsfile=8713. • "1999 Year-End Sales Reach All-Time High of $149 Billion," Semiconductor Industry Association, www.semichips.org/pre_ release.cfm?ID=176.

### IBM

Jonathan Martin, "International Business Machines Corporation," in *International Directory of Company Histories*, vol. 6, ed., Paula Kepos (Detroit: St. James Press, 1992), pp. 250–253. • "Background," IBM, www.ibm.com/press/background.phtml. • "IBM History Highlights," IBM," www.ibm.com/ibm/history/. • Robert Sobel, *IBM: Colossus in Transition* (New York: Times Books, 1981). • "The New IBM," *Business Week*, 16 December 1991. • "IBM Research," www.research.ibm.com/. • "Directory of Worldwide Contacts," IBM, www.ibm.com/ planetwide/. • IBM *Annual Report*, various years. • *Moody's Industrial Manual* (New York: Moody's Investors' Service, various years). • Emerson Pugh, *Building IBM: Shaping an Industry and Its Technology* (Cambridge, Mass.: MIT Press, 1995). • IBM 10-K Reports, various years, www.sec.gov. • *Directory of Corporate Affiliations* (New Providence, N.J.: National Register Publishing, 1999).

### Siemens

Beth Watson Highman, "Siemens AG," in *International Directory of Company Histories*, vol. 14, ed., Tina Grant (Detroit: St. James Press, 1996), pp. 444–447. • "Halfway There: Siemens," *The Economist*, 4 July 1992, p. 60. • Siemens AG *Annual Report*, various years. • Siemens Form 10-K various years, www.sec.gov. • *Siemens 1847–1997: Dates, Facts and Figures* (Munich: Corporate Communications,1997). • *International Directory of Corporate Affiliations* (New Providence, N.J.: National Register Publishing, 1999). • "Siemens Investor Relations," www.siemens.com/index.

### LG Electronics

"The World's Largest Corporations," *Fortune* 2000 Global 500. • "The Lucky–Goldstar Group," *Hoover's Handbook of World Business 1992* (Austin, Tex.: Reference Press, 1992), p. 228. • "LG Electronics Co., Ltd.," Wright Investor's Service, http://profiles.wisi.com/profiles/scripts/ corpinfo2.asp?cusip=C41008440. • "Corporate Chronology," LG Group, www.lge.co.kr/ english/IR/98/annual_chronology.html. • LG Electronics *Annual Report*, various years. • "Business Overview," LGE, www.lge.co.kr/english/IR/98/annual_overview.html. • "Investor Relations," LGE, www.lge.co.kr/english/IR/. • "LG Electronics Hits Homerun in Thailand with Localized Marketing," www.lg.co.kr/e_lg/about/news/newsflash/0003/000314-1.html.

## Software and the Internet

"Global Internet Statistics," www.globalreach.com/globalstats. • "How Many Online?" NUA, www.nua.ie/surveys. • "Statistics for Online Purchases," www.epaynews.com/statistics/ purchases.html. • "Most Global Corporations Recruit Online," e-gateway.net/infoarea/news/ news.cfm?nid=571. • "Measuring Electronic Commerce: International Trade in Software," www1.oecd.org/dsti/sti/it/ec/prod/sw-trade.htm. • "1999 Global Software Piracy Report," www.bsa.org/usa/globallib/piracy/piracystats99.phtml.

### Microsoft

"Microsoft Fast Facts," www.microsoft.com/presspass/fastfacts.htm. • "U.S. v. Microsoft: Proposed Findings of Fact," www.usdoj.gov/atr/cases/f2600/2613toc_htm.htm. • Philip Greenspun, "Bill Gates Personal Wealth Clock," www.webho.com/WealthClock. • Scott Lewis, "Microsoft Corporation," in *International Directory of Company Histories*, vol. 6, ed., Paula Kepos (Detroit: St. James Press, 1992), pp. 257–260. • Nathan Newman, "A Global Perspective on Microsoft," *Micro$oft Monitor*, 27 April 1998, www.netaction.org/monitor/. • J. Wallace, *Hard Drive: Bill Gates and the Making of the Microsoft Empire* (New York: Wiley, 1992). • "Microsoft Worldwide," www.microsoft.com/worldwide/. • Microsoft 10-K Reports, various years, www.sec.gov. • *Moody's OTC Manual* (New York: Moody's Investors' Service, various years).

## Telecommunications

"A Brief Overview of Global and Regional Trends in Telecommunications Infrastructure," www.apc.org/books/ictpolsa/app-1.htm#f2. • "Congress Should Uplink Competition," Matthew Lynch, http://reason.com/opeds/lynch032398.shtml. • "The World's Largest Corporations," *Fortune 2000 Global 500.* • "Telecom Agreement," http://europa.eu.int/ISPO/docs/services/newsletter/97/february/ISPOFEB02.html. • www.telegeography.com. • "Telecommunications," in Scott Heil, ed., *Encyclopedia of Global Industries* (Detroit: Gale, 1999).

### Verizon

Roger Rouland, "GTE Corporation," in *International Directory of Company Histories,* vol. 5, ed., Adele Hast (Detroit.: St. James Press, 1992), pp. 294–298. • Francis Norton, "Bell Atlantic," in *International Directory of Company Histories,* vol. 5, ed., Adele Hast (Detroit: St. James Press, 1992), pp. 272–275. • Verizon *Annual Report,* various years. • GTE, Bell Atlantic, and Verizon 10-K Reports, various years, www.sec.gov. • "About Verizon," www22.verizon.com/about/?loc=HH.

## Commercial Banking

"The World's Largest Corporations," *Fortune 2000 Global 500.* • "Central Bank Survey of Foreign Exchange and Derivatives Market Activity in April 2001: Preliminary Global Data," Bank for International Settlements, www.bis.org/press/p011009.pdf. • Richard Barnet and John Cavanagh, *Global Dreams: Imperial Corporations and the New World Order* (New York: Simon and Schuster, 1998), p. 386.

### Bank of Tokyo-Mitsubishi

Bank of Tokyo-Mitsubishi *Annual Report,* various years. • David Salamie, "Bank of Tokyo-Mitsubishi," in *International Directory of Company Histories,* vol. 15, ed., Tina Grant (Detroit: St. James Press, 1996), pp. 41–43. • "Tokyo-Mitsubishi, Bank of," *Encyclopaedia Britannica* Online Edition, www.britannica.com/. • "Bank of Tokyo-Mitsubishi, Ltd.," Hoover's Online, www.hoovers.com/co/capsule/0/0,2163,51170,00.html. • *Directory of Corporate Affiliations* (New Providence, N.J.: National Register Publishing, 1999). • "A Global Presence in Regional Markets," www.btm.co.jp/html_e/network/network.htm.

### Citibank

"Global Consumer Businesses," www.citigroup.com/citigroup/homepage/lob/sub/gconb/mid.htm. • Edna Hedblad and Susan Brown, "Citigroup Inc.," in *International Directory of Company Histories,* vol. 30, ed., Jay Pederson (Detroit: St. James Press, 2000), pp. 124–128. • Citigroup/Citibank 10-K Reports, various years, www.sec.gov. • *Moody's Banking and Finance Manual* (New York: Moody's Investors' Service, various years). • *Directory of Corporate Affiliations* (New Providence, N.J.: National Register Publishing, 1999). • Citibank *Annual Reports,* various years. • H. van Cleveland et al., *Citibank, 1812–1970* (Cambridge, Mass.: Harvard University Press, 1985). • "About Us," www.citigroup.com/. • *Directory of Corporate Affiliations* (New Providence, N.J.: National Register Publishing, 1999).

## Transportation and Postal Services

"The World's Largest Corporations," *Fortune 2000 Global 500.* • "Postal Services," in Scott Heil, ed., *Encyclopedia of Global Industries* (Detroit: Gale, 1999). • "Current Issues for Postal Workers," http://ilo.org/public/english/dialogue/sector/papers/factsheet/sep11_postal.htm. • "World Airline Industry Statistics," *Air Transport World,* July 2001, pp. 20–21.

## United Parcel Service (UPS)

"UPS Worldwide," http://pressroom.ups.com/worldwide/content/0,1012,,FF.html. • "Company History," http://pressroom.ups.com/about/history/0,1055,,00.html. • "UPS Facts: UPS General Company Information,"http://pressroom.ups.com/about/facts/0,1056,134,00.html. • UPS *Annual Report,* various years. • "UPS Wins Tentative Award of China Air Rights," www.ups.com/chinaairrights/news/lands.html. • Brian O'Reilly "They've Got Mail," *Fortune,* 7 February 2000. • "United Parcel Service," *Hoover's Handbook of Private Business* (Austin, Tex.: Reference Press, various years). • "Worldwide Delivery Times," wwwapps.ups.com/servlet/WWDTServlet?IATA=us&Lang=eng.

### British Airways

"BA Fact Book 2000: British Airways Profile," www.britishairways.com/inside/ir/factbook/section_2.doc. • David Walsh, "Concorde—Its History and Tragedy," 28 July 2000, www.wsws.org/articles/2000/jul2000/con1-j28.shtml. • "British Airways," *Hoover's Handbook of World Business* (Austin, Tex.: Reference Press, 1999). • "Concorde," www.britishairways.com/flights/flyus/concorde/concorde.shtml. • British Airways *Annual Report,* various years. • *Directory of Corporate Affiliations* (New Providence, N.J.: National Register Publishing, 1999).

## Legal Services

"Legal Services," in Scott Heil, ed., *Encyclopedia of Global Industries* (Detroit: Gale, 1999). • "The Battle of the Atlantic," *The Economist,* 26 February 2000.

### White & Case

"The Battle of the Atlantic," *The Economist,* 26 February 2000, p. 79. • "Who's Going Global," *The American Lawyer,* November 2000. • "A Global Law Firm," www.whitecase.com/practices.html. • "The Practice Areas of White & Case LLP," www.whitecase.com/overview.html. • "White & Case LLP: The Scoop—Building an International Power," The Vault Online, www.vault.com/companies/reports/. • White & Case LLP *Annual Report,* various years.

## Food and Food Services

Richard Barnet and John Cavanagh, *Global Dreams: Imperial Corporations and the New World Order* (New York: Simon and Schuster, 1994), pp. 208–232. • "Top 400 Restaurant Concepts," www.rimag.com. • Ronald Wirtz, "A Borderless Perspective," *fedgazette,* January 2000, p.15. • "Restaurants," in Scott Heil, ed., *Encyclopedia of Global Industries* (Detroit: Gale, 1999).

### Nestlé

Richard Barnet and John Cavanagh, *Global Dreams: Imperial Corporations and the New World Order* (New York: Simon and Schuster, 1994), p. 222. • Anne C. Hughes, "Nestlé, SA," in *International Directory of Company Histories,* vol. 7, ed., Paula Kepos (Detroit: St. James Press, 1993), pp. 380–384. • "Can Nestlé Be the Very Best?" *Fortune,* 13 November 2000, p. 353. • "Investor Relations," www.nestle.com/investor_relations/. • Nestlé, SA, *This Is Your Company,* 1946. • *Moody's Industrial Manual* (New York: Moody's Investors' Service, various years). • Nestlé *Annual Report,* various years. • "Nestlé," *Hoover's Handbook of World Business* (Austin, Tex.: Reference Press, 1992). • "Worldwide Addresses," www.nestle.com/all_about/ww_address/index.htm.

## Advertising

"Advertising Agencies," in Scott Heil, ed., *Encyclopedia of Global Industries* (Detroit: Gale, 1999). ● "Sparkling Slogan Is Century's Gem," www.suntimes.co.za/1999/04/25/insight/in06.htm. ● "Advertising Industry Ensnarled in the Perfect Storm," www.aded.org. ● "World's Top 100 Advertising Organizations," http://adage.com/dataplace/archives/dp444.html.

"Saatchi & Saatchi," www.hoovers.com. ● "Saatchi & Saatchi," Marketing Information Net Directory, www.mind-advertising.com/uk/ssgrp_uk.htm. ● "Saatchi & Saatchi," *Hoover's Handbook of World Business* (Austin, Tex.: Reference Press, 1992), p. 277. ● "Saatchi & Saatchi PLC," in *International Directory of Company Histories*, vol. 1, ed., Thomas Derdak (Detroit: St. James Press, 1988), pp. 33–35. ● "Saatchi & Saatchi," Marketing Information Net Directory, www.mind-advertising.com/uk/ssgrp_uk.htm ● Saatchi & Saatchi *Annual Report*, various years ● "Our Network," www.saatchi-saatchi.com/linkpage/index.html#.

## Media and Entertainment

Robert McChesney, "The Political Economy of Global Media," www.wacc.org.uk/media/mcchesney.htm. ● AOL Time Warner *2000 Annual Report*. ● "The World's Largest Corporations," *Fortune 2000 Global 500*.

### Bertelsmann

"Bertelsmann Chronicles," www.bertelsmann.com/facts/chronic/chronic.cfm. ● Dirk Bavendamm, "Bertelsmann AG," in *International Directory of Company Histories*, vol. 15, ed., Tina Grant (Detroit: St. James Press, 1996), pp. 51–54. ● "Bertelsmann AG," in *Hoover's Handbook of World Business* (Austin, Tex.: Reference Press, 1999), p. 122. ● "Investor Relations," www.bertelsmann.com/index.cfm. ● *Directory of Corporate Affiliations* (New Providence, N.J.: National Register Publishing, 1999).

### AOL Time Warner

"Investor Relations," www.corp.aol.com/ir. ● Diane Mermigas, "Time Warner Inc.," in *International Directory of Company Histories*, vol. 7, ed., Paula Kepos (Detroit: St. James Press, 1993), pp. 526–530. ● Elizabeth Rourke "America Online, Inc.," in *International Directory of Company Histories*, vol. 10, ed., Paula Kepos (Detroit: St. James Press, 1995), pp. 56–58. ● America Online, AOL Factbook, October 1999. ● Stephen Labaton, "AOL and Time Warner Gain Approval for Huge Merger, but with Strict Conditions," *New York Times*, 15 December 2000. p. A1. ● "Historical Dates for America Online," http://corp.aol.com/who_timeline.html. ● AOL, Inc. 10-K Reports, various years, www.sec.gov. ● "International Access Numbers," http://intlaccess.web.aol.com/.

## Consulting and Accounting

"Management Consultancy," *The Economist*, 22 March 1997. ● www.kennedyinfo.com/mc/cn50.html. ● www.accountancyage.com/top50. ● www.mca.org.uk/feacosurvey.pdf. ● http://proquest.com.

### Arthur Andersen/Accenture

Thomas Derdak and Sheila Brown, "Andersen Worldwide," in *International Directory of Company Histories*, vol. 29, ed., Tina Grant (Detroit: St. James Press, 2000),pp. 25–27. ● "Arthur Andersen & Co," *Hoover's Handbook of World Business* (Austin, Tex.: Reference Press, 1992), p. 152. ● *Arthur Andersen: The First 60 Years: 1913–1973*, 1973. ● "Andersen's Android Wars," *The Economist*, 12 August 2000, p. 64. ● "About Us: Culture," www.arthurandersen.com/website.nsf.content/AboutUsCulture?OpenDocument. ● "About Us: Score Card," www.arthurandersen.com/website.nsf.content/AboutUsScoreCard?OpenDocument. ● "Accenture," Hoover's Online, www.hoovers.com/co/capsule/6/0,2163,43516,00.html. ● "Our Capabilities: Consulting," www.accenture.com/xd/xd.asp?it=enWeb&xd=about\us%5Ccapabilities%5Ccapa_consulting.xml. ● Accenture 10-K Reports, various years, www.sec.gov. ● "Facts and Figures," www.sec.gov. ● "Our Offices," http://ac.com/locations/loca_home.html.

## Retail

"The World's Largest Corporations," *Fortune 2000 Global 500*. ● "U.S. Retailers Dominate While Globalization Decelerates," PriceWaterhouseCoopers Press Release, August 2000. ● "Retail Department Stores," in Scott Heil, ed., *Encyclopedia of Global Industries* (Detroit: Gale, 1999).

### Wal-Mart

Carol Healy, "Wal-Mart Stores, Inc." in *International Directory of Company Histories*, vol. 8, ed., Jay Pederson (Detroit: St. James Press, 1999), pp. 525–557. ● High Ridge Homeowners Association, "A Position Paper Opposing the Proposed Rezoning for an Atlanta Highway Wal-Mart Supercenter," www.fivepts.com/westside.htm#business. ● "Wal-Mart International," www.walmartstores.com/supplier/vstand. ● "Wal-Mart Dungeon in China," http://nclnet.org/report 00/walmart.htm. ● A. Bernstein and D. Roberts, "A Life of Fines and Beatings," *Business Week*, 2 October 2000, pp. 122–128. ● "Investor Relations," http://investor.walmartstores.com/ireye/ir_site.zhtml?ticker=wmt&script=2100. ● *Moody's Service Manual* (New York: Moody's Investors' Service, various years).

## V. The Impacts of Multinational Corporations

1. Eric Kolodner, *Transnational Corporations: Impediments or Catalysts of Social Development*, Occasional Paper no. 5, World Summit for Social Development.

2. UNCTAD, *World Investment Report 1999*, p. 265.

3. United Nations Transnational Corporations and Management Division, *World Investment Report 1992* (New York: United Nations, 1992), p. 186. Indirect employment generated by transnational corporations is at least twice that generated by direct employment; indirect employment includes jobs produced by purchasing goods and services from local suppliers and subcontractors and providing resources that can be used in further production within a host country.

4. "The World's Largest Corporations," *Fortune 2000 Global 500*.

5. UNCTAD, *World Investment Report 1994*, pp. 4–5.

6. UNCTAD, *World Investment Report 1999*.

7. Organization for Economic Cooperation and Development, *Globalization and Environment: Preliminary Perspectives*, Business and Industry Advisory Committee Discussion Paper, 1997.

8. UNCTAD, *World Investment Report 1994*, p. 32.

9. UNCTAD, *World Investment Report 1999*, p.166.

10. U.S Department of Commerce, *Direct Investment Abroad: 1994 Benchmark Survey Final Results* (Washington, D.C.: U.S. Department of Commerce, 1994), Table III. J. 1.

11. United Nations Transnational Corporations and Management Division, *World Investment Report 1992* (New York: United Nations, 1992).

12. "Gimme Shelter," *The Economist*, 29 January 2000, p. 17.

13. Ibid., p. 21.

14. UNCTAD, *World Investment Report 1999*, p. 167.

15. Robert McIntyre and T. D. Coo Nguyen, *Corporate Income Taxes in the 1990s* (Washington, D.C.: Institute on Taxation and Economic Policy, 2000).
16. "Enron's Reach," *Philadelphia Enquirer*, 31 January 2002, p. A7. Compiled from Enron Corp. and SEC data.
17. "Less Than Zero: Enron's Income Tax Payments, 1996–2000," Citizens for Tax Justice, www.ctj.org/html/enron.htm.
18. United Nations Development and Human Rights Section, *Development Update* no. 27 (New York, April 1999).
19. UNCTAD, *World Investment Report 1999*, p. 199.
20. John Cantwell, "The Globalization of Technology: What Remains of the Product Cycle Model?" *Cambridge Journal of Economics* 19, no. 1, pp. 155–174. As cited in UNCTAD, *World Investment Report 1999*, p. 200.
21. UNCTAD, *World Investment Report 1999*, p. 201.
22. "Patents Registered in the U.S." is used as an overall measure of innovation; inventions are patented in many countries, but the U.S. is a primary market where inventions tend to be patented consistently.
23. UNCTAD, *World Investment Report 1999*, p. 215.
24. United Nations Conference on Trade and Development, *The World Investment Report 1999: Foreign Direct Investment and the Challenge of Development* (New York: United Nations, 1999), p. xvi.
25. United Nations Development and Human Rights Section, *Development Update* no. 27.
26. Joseph Yam, "International Capital Flows and Free Markets," www.info.gov.hk/hkma/engl/speechs/joseph/speech_260399b.htm
27. Robert McChesney, "The Political Economy of Global Media," www.wacc/org.uk/media/mcchesney.htm.
28. "2001 Country Listing," www.mcdonalds.com/corporate/investor/financialinfo/systemrest/index.html.
29. Gary Gardner, "People Everywhere Eating More Fast Foods," in *Vital Signs, 1999*, ed., Linda Starke (New York: W. W. Norton, 1999), pp. 150–151.
30. "McDonald's World Wide Corporate Site," www.mcdonalds.com/corporate/index.html.
31. Ibid.
32. McDonald's *Annual Report*, various years.
33. "McDonald's Country Specific Websites," www.mcdonalds.com/countries/index.html.
34. McDonald's *Annual Report*, various years.
35. "The World's View of Multinationals," p. 21.
36. UNCTAD, *Environmental Management in Transnational Corporations: Report on the Benchmark Corporate Environmental Survey* (Geneva: United Nations, 1993).
37. Joshua Karliner, *The Corporate Planet: Ecology and Politics in the Age of Globalization* (San Francisco: Sierra Club Books, 1997).
38. Arjun Makhijani et al., *Climate Change and Transnational Corporations Analysis and Trends* (New York: United Nations, 1992).
39. United Nations Conference on Transnational Corporations, *Transnational Corporations and Issues Relating to the Environment: The Contribution of the Commission and UNCTC to the Work of the Preparatory Committee of the UN Conference on Environment and Development* (New York: United Nations, 1991).
40. GEMI, *Fostering Environmental Prosperity: Multinationals in Developing Countries*.
41. "The World's View of Multinationals," p. 21.
42. UNCTAD, *World Investment Report 1999*, p. 299.

43. Ibid., p. 302.
44. Hilary French, *Vanishing Borders: Protecting the Planet in the Age of Globalization* (New York: W. W. Norton, 2000).
45. "The Fun of Being a Multinational," p. 21.

## Figure and Map Sources

"Employment by Multinational Corporations 1975–1998" and "Employees in Foreign Affiliates As a Percentage of Total Number of Employees in Country 1985–1995": UNCTAD, *World Investment Report 1999*, pp. 265–266. ● "Employment in U.S. Multinational Corporations' Foreign Affiliates 1997": Bureau of Economic Affairs, "U.S. Multinational Companies: Operations in 1997," www.bea.doc.gov/bea/ai/0799mnc/maintext.htm. ● "Major Global Tax Havens": www.taxscape.com. ● "Enron Subsidiaries": See note 18, chapter 5. ● "Effective Tax Rate & Profits of 250 Large U.S. Corporations 1981–1998": See note 17, chapter 5. ● "Share of U.S. Patents Registered by the World's Largest Firms Attributable to Research in Foreign Locations 1969–1995": UNCTAD, *World Investment Report 1999*, p. 200. ● "Percentage of National R&D Financing from Private Industry Latest Available Year": National Science Foundation, "National Patterns of R&D Resources: 1998," www.nsf.gov/sbe/srs/nsf99335/htmstart.htm. ● "Ratio of Corporate and Federal R&D Expenditures in the United States 1953–1999": National Science Foundation, "Total R&D by Industry 1953–1999," http://caspar.nsf.gov/nsf/srs/IndRD/start.htm. ● "World's Largest Financial Firms Market Capitalization": "Crisis? What Crisis?" *The Economist*, 16 May 2002, p. 76. ● "Inward Foreign Direct Investment As Percentage of GDP by Country/Region 1997" and "Inward Foreign Direct Investment by Region/Country 1997": UNCTAD, *World Investment Report 1999*, p. 513. ● "National Foreign Investment Regulatory Changes 1991–1997": UNCTAD, *World Investment Report 1999*, p. 115. ● "Number of Restaurants by Country/Territory" and "Number of Restaurants by Region 2000,": www.mcdonalds.com/corporate/investor/financialinfo/systemrest/index.html. ● "Number of Restaurants Built 1995–2000," "U.S. vs. Rest of World Restaurants 1980–2000," and "Regional Sales 2000,": McDonald's *Annual Report*, various years. ● "$CO_2$ Emitted Annually by Country, Company, or Continent": See note 1, Introduction. ● "Examples of Environmental Impacts of Multinational Corporations": Los Angeles, "Doing Well by Doing Solar," www.edcmag.com/CDA/ArticleInformation/features/BNP__Features__Item/0,4120,21258,00.html; Torreón, "Mexico: Communities Win Against Silver Producing Giant," www.corpwatch.org/issues/PID.jsp2articleid=802; Aberdeen, "The Weyerhaeuser Story," http://grp.enviroweb.org/corporat.htm; Maracaibo, "Contribution of Trade to Environmental Performance and Sustainable Development," www.cefic.be/position/icca/pp_ic024.htm; Nigeria, "Oil Bringing Untold Damage to Niger Delta," http://archive.greenpeace.org/~comms/ken/onsla001.html; Brazil and Spain, See note 3, chapter 5; Brent Spar, "Greenpeace Brent Spar Protest in the North Sea," http://archive.greenpeace.org/~comms/brent/brent.html; Bhopal, "Bhopal," www.bhopal.com; Indonesia, "Freeport McMoRan: Environmental Issues," www.moles.org/ProjectUnderground/motherlode/freeport/env.html. ● "Privatization Revenues": UNCTAD, *World Investment Report 2000*, p. 132. ● "Number of ISO 14001 Certifications Awarded by Country 1995–1999": "The ISO Survey of ISO 9000 and 14000 Certificates," www.iso.org/iso/en/prods-services/otherpubs/pdf/survey11thcycle.pdf.

## VI. The Governance of Multinational Corporations

1. "A Tussle over Tax," *The Economist*, 4 March 2000, p. 67; "Airbus Bets the Company," *The Economist*, 18 March 2000, p. 75; "Foreign sales corporations" are tax-avoidance vehicles for U.S.-based exporters that are worth $3.5 billion to $4 billion per year to U.S. export-ers. Boeing alone "saved" $130 million in taxes in 1998, and GE $150 million. Some 6,000 U.S. firms benefit from this scheme. The WTO has ruled these shell companies in offshore tax havens to be tax-avoidance vehicles and illegal export subsidies to firms based in the U.S.

2. Eric Kolodner, *Transnational Corporations: Impediments or Catalysts of Social Develop-ment*, Occasional Paper no. 5, World Summit for Social Development.

3. David Malakoff, "Nigerian Families Sue Pfizer, Testing the Reach of U.S. Law," *Science* 293 (September 7, 2001), p. 1742.

4. Department of Public International Law, "Multinational Corporations and Human Rights," Erasmus University, www.multinationals.law.eur.nl/documents/colloquium062299.html.

5. "Go Global, Sue Local," *The Economist*, 14 August 1999, p. 54.

6. Alexandre Kiss and Dianah Shelton, *International Environmental Law*, 2nd ed., (New York: Transnational Publishers, 2000).

7. Bela Balanya, et.al., *Europe, Inc.: Regional and Global Restructuring and the Rise of Corporate Power* (London: Pluto Press, 2000).

8. Dalip S. Swamy, *Multinational Corporations and the World Economy* (New Delhi: Alps Publishers, 1980), p. 130.

9. "The Case for Brands," *The Economist*, 8 September 2001, p. 11.

10. Chris Marsden, foreword to *Global Corporate Citizenship—Rationale and Strategies*, by David Logan, et al. (Washington, D.C.: Hitachi Foundation, 1999).

11. "Researchers Investigate Stakeholder and Shareholder Value," *Business and the Environment*, September 2000.

12. Chris Marsden, foreword to *Global Corporate Citizenship—Rationale and Strategies*.

13. Foundation Center, *Foundation Center Giving Yearbook* (Washington, D.C.: Foundation Center, 1999).

14. Eric Kolodner, *Transnational Corporations: Impediments or Catalysts of Social Development?*

15. Harlan Cleveland, "Corporate Diplomacy," *The World Paper*, February 1993, p. 1.

16. "Best Behaviors," *The Economist*, 14 July 2001, p. 71.

17. "Japan's Corporate-Governance U-turn," *The Economist*, 18 November 2000, p. 73.

18. The U.S. alone had more than 1.1 million nongovernmental organizations in 1998. *Global Corporate Citizenship—Rationale and Strategies*.

19. Alan Croswell, "Advocates Gain Ground in a Globalized Era," *New York Times*, 18 December 2000, p. C19.

20. Kenny Bruno, Joshua Karliner, and China Brotsky, *Greenhouse Gangsters vs. Environmental Justice* (San Francisco: CorpWatch, 1999).

21. Tom Jones, et al., "Pollution for Export?" *The UNESCO Courier*, December 1998.

22. "Helping but Not Developing," *The Economist*, 12 May 2001, p. 52.

23. "The Fun of Being a Multinational," p. 21.

24. Michael Shuman, "Gattzilla v. Communities," *Cornell International Law Journal* 27, no. 3 (1994), pp. 12–15.

25. Joseph Kahn, "Multinationals Sign UN Pact on Rights and Environment," *New York Times*, 27 July 2001, p.3.

26. "Firm Resolutions," *The Economist*, 12 May 2001, p. 64.

27. Eric Kolodner, *Transnational Corporations: Impediments or Catalysts of Social Development?*

28. Robert Kuttner, "The Role of Governments in the Global Economy," in *Global Capitalism*, eds., Will Hutton and Anthony Giddens (New York: The New Press, 2000), p. 50.

29. "Roasting an Old Chestnut," *The Economist*, 8 October 2001, p. 81.

30. "Performance Track Intrigues Academics," *International Environmental Systems Update*, November 2000, p. 4.

31. United Nations Centre on Transnational Corporations, 1990, in Eric Kolodner, *Transnational Corporations: Impediments or Catalysts of Social Development?*

32. BP's CEO pledged in 2002 at the Davos World Economic Forum that it had ceased all corporate contributions to political campaigns around the world.

33. Richard H. Friman, ed., *The Illicit Global Economy and State Power* (Oxford, UK: Rowman and Littlefield, 1999).

34. Clifton Leaf, "Send Them to Jail: It's Time to Stop Coddling White Collar Crooks," *Fortune*, 18 March 2002.

35. John Eatwell and Lance Taylor, *Global Finance at Risk: The Case for International Regulations* (New York: The New Press, 2000).

Figure and Map Sources
"Number of Nationalizations in Selected Developing Countries 1960–1992" and "Distribution of Nationalizations by Sector 1960–1992": Stephen Kobrin, "Foreign Enterprise and Forced Divestment in LDCs," *International Organization* 34 (Winter 1980) and data updates from Kobrin. ● "Number of Privatizations by Region 1980–1993": "Trends in Privatization," www.cipe.org/ert/e27/shirle27.php3. ● "Company Environmental Rating vs. Stock Performance": See note 3, chapter 5.

# Index